# THE
# HOGAN
# WAY

## Also by John Andrisani

*The Nicklaus Way*
*The Bobby Jones Way*
*The Tiger Woods Way*

# THE HOGAN WAY

## HOW TO APPLY BEN HOGAN'S EXCEPTIONAL SWING AND SHOTMAKING GENIUS TO YOUR OWN GAME

# John Andrisani

## HarperResource

*An Imprint of HarperCollinsPublishers*

HarperCollins books may be purchased for educational, business, or sales promotional use. For information, please write to: Special Markets Department, HarperCollins Publishers Inc., 10 East 53rd Street, New York, NY 10022.

First HarperResource paperback edition published in 2004.

*Designed by Stanley S. Drate/Folio Graphics Co. Inc.*

The Library of Congress has catalogued the hardcover edition as follows:
Andrisani, John.
    The Hogan way : how to apply Ben Hogan's exceptional swing and shotmaking genius to your own game / John Andrisani.
        p. cm.
    ISBN 0-06-270236-X
    1. Swing (Golf)  2. Hogan, Ben, 1912–  I. Title.
GV979.S9 A52 2000
796.352'3—dc21                                                        99-049837
    ISBN 0-06-273660-4 (pbk.)

04 05 06 07 08 FG/RRD 10 9 8 7 6 5 4 3 2 1

*I dedicate this book to the millions of golfers
who possess the potential to play a
better game but are lost because of
instructional misinformation.*

# Contents

# Acknowledgments

This book would not have come together had it not been for the help of others.

I thank my agent, Scott Waxman of the Scott Waxman Agency, and Robert Wilson, former senior editor at HarperCollins Publishers, for believing in and supporting my idea to write a book that unravels the mystery behind the machinelike swing technique of golfing legend Ben Hogan.

I'm grateful for the rare photographs contained in this book. I was very lucky to acquire such technically revealing instructional "takes" of Hogan swinging, especially those taken by Leonard Kamsler and the late Chuck Brenkus. I also thank Corbis, a New York–based photographic library, for digging out of their archives some wonderful photographs that show Hogan hitting a variety of shots.

I also thank artist Shu Kuga for doing such a first-class job of visually communicating Hogan's vital setup and swing techniques to readers like you.

I thank participating instructors from *GOLF Magazine*'s top one hundred teachers in America list, and also the knowledgeable members of the United States Golf Teachers Federation for their insightful remarks on Hogan's superlative swing. I also express my gratitude to the tour professionals, television golf commentators, members of the golf press, and talented amateurs, for their views on this great man and his method.

Special thanks go to the Shell Oil Company for the video they produced showing the Hogan versus Snead match that took place at the Houston Country Club in Houston, Texas, in May 1964. Every golfer should have this in his library of tapes. Seeing Hogan in action, hitting every single fairway and green, on his way to shooting a winning score of 69, made me more enthusiastic about writing *The Hogan Way*, plus it provided me with such close-up glimpses of his swing that I found it easier to analyze his secrets.

I thank Lana, a superb painter and pianist, and most of all a wonderful person, for making my life so much less stressful during the preparation of what I truly believe is a one-of-a-kind instructional book.

I thank Ken Bowden, the supremely talented golf editor and writer, who many years ago taught me the art of putting across, on paper, the instructional message.

Last, I thank the late William Benjamin Hogan for leaving such a legacy. Hogan was not only the best ball-striker of all time, but also so polished a person that he kept golf a gentleman's game—throughout his illustrious career and forever, always.

# Introduction

J ack, Lee, Snead, Nelson, Sarazen, Venturi, Els, Duval—all great players who are referred to by their first or last names. There are other golf professionals, past and present, who go by a friendlier form of their first name. Examples: Bobby, for Bobby Jones, Arnie for Arnold Palmer, or Freddie for Fred Couples. And those that are called by their middle name. Case in point: Tiger. When one player's name comes up, and only that player's, he is called Mr.—Mr. Hogan to be exact.

There are sundry reasons why Ben Hogan—the man who had the most influence on golfing techniques since Bobby Jones—is put on a pedestal. Hogan's ball-striking ability was so precise that he literally wore down the grooves in the "sweet spot" of the clubface. No player, past or present, struck the ball so purely. When Hogan's club hit the ball, the sound of impact was like no other, sort of a supersonic hissing sound. What's more, Hogan was so talented that, during his hot years on tour, onlookers believed he was capable of shooting as low a score as was needed to win.

Hogan concentrated so intently on the golf course that when contemplating a shot, he looked long and hard at the target, working out every angle in his head while puffing on his ever-present cigarette. On more than one occasion, at a tournament venue, "The Hawk" looked right through his own wife Valerie with his steely ice-blue eyes, as if she were merely a stranger in the gallery. There's no doubt that Timothy Gallwey, Bob Rotella, and other mental gurus help golfers think their way to lower scores. But it was the stoic Hogan who first learned to play according to the mind-over-matter philosophy.

No professional practiced more diligently than Hogan, particularly during his early days as a pro, when he started working extra hard to change a bad swing into a flowing, easy-to-repeat action. Hogan hit so many practice balls that the palms of his hands turned leathery, and sometimes even bled.

No player was more determined than Hogan, either, mainly because he had to overcome the obstacles of growing up poor and losing a father to suicide. Because Hogan was not a natural like his contemporary Sam Snead, he spent hours on the practice tee developing a swing he could depend on. Furthermore, Hogan was at a huge disadvantage owing to a serious duck-hook problem that made him a slow starter. But the slender and slight Hogan never gave up, even though for several years on tour he lived pretty much like a hobo. This former caddy, who started golf swinging a rustic hickory-shafted five-iron, traveled to tournaments in a virtual jalopy, stayed in cheap roadside hotels, and ate greasy-spoon meals.

Once he joined the tour in 1930, Hogan arrived very early at each tournament site, giving himself ample time before the round to hit a variety of clubs in his bag, starting with the nine-iron. He would not usually switch clubs until he had mastered the one in his hands. Hogan was also the innovator of postround practice. At first, Hogan's fellow competitors laughed at him for hitting balls after a round. But as soon as Hogan's game started to improve markedly, they jumped off their 19th-hole barstools and followed the Texan's example, hitting golf shots rather than drinking shots of whiskey.

Hogan did not win a tournament single-handedly until 1940. That year he broke through winning three events in a row, starting with the North-South, which back then was considered a major championship. Hogan's run of success continued. He was the leading money winner in 1940, 1941, 1942, 1946, and 1948. Between 1930 and 1948, he also won the 1946 PGA championship, plus the 1948 PGA and U.S. Open championships. Hogan also played on the 1941 and 1947 Ryder Cup teams and was undefeated in his matches.

Hogan's run of success came to an abrupt halt in 1949, due to a near-fatal automobile accident. Following almost a year of recovery time, this resilient former Army Air Corps lieutenant went on to do great things, things no other golfer has ever accomplished. Hogan won a number of regular tour events, but his most noted achievements included wins at the 1950 and 1951 U.S. Open, and the 1951 Masters. As if saving himself for something special, Hogan did not win any of the four major titles in 1952, but was unstoppable the following year. In 1953, Hogan won three major championships:

the Masters, the U.S. Open, and the PGA. The bottom line: this tough Texan truly earned the Mr. Hogan moniker, and was deserving of the ticker-tape parade given in his honor in 1953.

In the same way that magicians are intrigued by Houdini, golfers look to Hogan (who died in 1997 with 63 PGA Tour events under his belt) as the ultimate golfing genius; the most skillful swinger and shotmaker of all time. Golfers are so intrigued by Hogan that whenever *GOLF Magazine* or *Golf Digest* features a story on this golfing great, sales skyrocket. The same success holds true for his books. Hogan's first instructional book, *Power Golf*, has been reprinted several times since its 1948 publication. Hogan's classic, *Five Lessons: The Modern Fundamentals of Golf*, originally published in 1957, remains the all-time best-selling instructional book.

When *Power Golf* was published, Hogan was playing winning golf. Nevertheless, his game had not peaked yet because of some serious faults in his swing. Hogan held the club with a strong grip, employed an overly long, very loose backswing, cleared his hips too soon on the downswing, and exaggerated the releasing action of the hands, arms, and club. A severe right-to-left hook shot was Hogan's bad shot. The fact that Hogan won tournaments with this handicap tells you that he was a superb trouble player, an excellent short-game scrambler, and an excellent putter. Still, because Hogan's swing was anything but mechanically sound, what he wrote in *Power Golf* has done golfers more harm than good.

In conducting research for *The Hogan Way*, I interviewed golfers who had read *Power Golf*. The majority of players who heeded Hogan's instructions hit slice shots. After swinging the club on the same backswing plane as Hogan, they confessed to having difficulty squaring the clubface at impact. The best they could do was return the club to the ball with its face open. Only the stronger and flexible players hooked the ball violently, just like Hogan. As a former golf teacher and instruction editor of *GOLF Magazine* for 16 years, I would advise against heeding the words Hogan wrote in that book. Frankly, if Hogan were alive today, I believe he would give the same advice, because his later swing bore little resemblance to his earlier swing. Hogan's earlier swing produced an uncontrollable hook, his later swing a super-controlled fade. So that you can learn from Hogan mistakes and have some good reference points for improving your swing, I will review Hogan's original swing in the opening chapter of this book.

*Five Lessons* is a wonderfully written book, owing to the stylish writing of Herbert Warren Wind, a true master of the English language and former golf writer for *Sports Illustrated* and *The New Yorker*. There are some technical elements contained in the text that you should consider copying. I'll review these in chapter two. Having said that, there are also some instructional points in *Five Lessons* that I believe are false. Moreover, there are some critically important elements of Hogan's setup and swing that go unmentioned, either because Hogan was unaware of them, or because he wanted to be secretive. Allow me to back up my points with some examples.

In *Five Lessons* Hogan tells golfers to begin the down-swing by turning the hips back to the left, the faster the better. No wonder so many recreational golfers come over the top, and either hook the ball or hit a pull slice. Hogan himself did not employ the hip action he recommended, as you will see when looking at the illustrations in chapter two and the sequence of photographs in chapter three. Shifting the hips laterally was Hogan's first move on the downswing, which is an action that prevents you from coming over the top.

An example of what Hogan did, but failed to mention in *Five Lessons*, involves the setup. Hogan set up with a closed stance—right foot back farther from the target line than the left. This is one of his "lost fundamentals," a true secret that will be reviewed in chapter two.

In this book, I analyze Hogan's swing down to the bare bones. This in-depth study will allow you to improve at a much faster rate than you have been accustomed to, simply because I separate fact from fiction. Thanks to help from top teachers and tour pros, friends and contemporaries of Hogan's, Hogan's former personal assistant, television golf analysts, and a lucky lady who received a lesson from the wizard himself, I tap into the talent of a shotmaking genius, the purest striker of a golf ball that ever lived. The end result: I will make you understand, once and for all, how you can apply the secrets of Hogan's setup and swing to your own game when you are swinging technologically advanced clubs featuring extra-long graphite shafts, oversized titanium heads, and less-lofted clubfaces.

Some of the many individuals whose expert commentary on Hogan's method is incorporated into *The Hogan Way* are: Ken Venturi, CBS golf analyst and longtime personal friend of Hogan's; Butch Harmon, Tiger Woods's coach who at age 12 played with Hogan; golfing legend and rival Sam Snead; Debbie Rivers, a Louisiana-based golfer to whom Hogan gave a lesson at Shady Oaks Country Club near Fort Worth, Texas; and Greg Hood, a former personal assistant of Hogan's who often watched and analyzed the practice habits of this golfing genius. I, too, share what I learned, in 1988, at the Waldorf Astoria Hotel in New York City, where Hogan was being honored by *GOLF Magazine* as one of golf's 100 heroes of the century.

The presentation of this instructional book is like no other golf book. That's because I trace the history of Hogan's masterful swing. I show you what you can learn from his mistakes and what aspects of his swing are well worth copying to the letter. I tell you how Hogan turned his game around, thanks to two simple lessons from golf professionals Henry Picard and Harry Cooper, and through tireless practice. Most importantly, I reveal secrets about Hogan's technique that have never been revealed by him or anyone else, and teach you how to hit the power-fade, Hogan's bread-and-butter shot.

My chief goal in *The Hogan Way* is to present the best aspects of Hogan's setup and swing—telling you what to copy and what not to copy—so that ultimately you will hit the ball more powerfully and accurately, will keep your good swing grooved, and will learn to hit a variety of shots well.

What further sets this book apart from the others are the photographs and artwork that help unravel the mystery of Hogan's swing, including a rare swing sequence of Hogan taken by Chuck Brenkus, the late golf photographer, friend of Hogan's, and Howard Hughes's golf instructor.

There is also a 16-page color insert, containing additional rare color photographs of Hogan. These candid "shots," taken by world-renowned golf photographer Leonard Kamsler, show Hogan preparing to play a shot, swinging full out with a driver, concentrating between shots, hitting approach shots with irons, chipping, putting, and practicing. Other photographs gathered from the archives of Corbis will help you to understand more clearly the ins and outs of Hogan's shotmaking techniques. The lucid and lifelike illustrations done by Japanese artist Shu Kuga further help relay the instructional message.

The ever-popular aforementioned instructional book by Hogan, *Five Lessons*, only focused on his full swing. Readers were not told how to score. Every golfer wants to lower his or her handicap, and that will not happen unless you have a great understanding of how to hit chips, pitches, sand shots, and other shots that require different techniques. In *The Hogan Way*, I analyze Hogan's total game and thus teach you the secrets he depended on to shave strokes off his score.

Practicing the right way is also vital to shooting lower scores. Hogan was the prime example of a player who did not just "beat balls," but practiced with a purpose. In chapter four of *The Hogan Way*, Hogan's well-thought-out practice habits are revealed through words and pictures.

The mental side is also critical to becoming a complete golfer. Insights into Hogan's golfing mind and his unique course-management skills accompany the insert photographs and are included in chapter five.

Reading *The Hogan Way* will help you sort out the confusion about Hogan's swing and shotmaking techniques. This book puts the legendary Hogan method into the proper context, so let it be your new guidebook to improvement.

JOHN ANDRISANI
*Orlando, Florida*

# 1

## Rocky Roads

•

### Learn from Hogan's early mistakes

In 1924, when William Benjamin Hogan was 12 years old, he caddied at the Glen Garden Country Club, near his home in Fort Worth, Texas.

Driving contests were a common thing around the caddy-yard, with each "looper" wanting to prove his machismo. Hogan did not fare too well in these competitions for a couple of reasons. First, he was short and skinny. Second, he used a cross-handed grip, employed by reversing the hands on the club so that the right hand is closer to the top of the handle. This grip is not recommended by golf teachers because it promotes an exaggerated hand action. When you become "handsy," as Hogan was to discover, the tendency is to pick up the club too quickly in the takeaway (the initial stage of the swing). In turn, this abrupt lifting action prevents you from shifting your weight properly on the backswing and disrupts the turning action of the body. So power is drained from the swing. Additionally, this highly un-orthodox grip gives you such little security in the left hand that you are unable to guide the club into the ball at impact. Hogan found out the hard way that clubhead speed alone is not what produces power. For maximum distance, the clubface must also make clean contact with the ball at impact, and to do that the left hand must be able to lead. When you use a cross-handed grip, it is ex-tremely difficult for you to attain control over the club. Consequently, the toe or heel end of the clubhead, rather than the sweet spot (located in the virtual center of the clubface), contacts the ball. Weak, off-line shots result.

Hogan wanted to win these driving contests so badly that he happily heeded the advice given to him by Ted Longworth, the pro at "The Garden." According to Curt Sampson, in *Hogan*, his absolutely must-read biography, this is what Longworth said: "Bennie, if you don't change that hog-killer's grip, you may as well take up cattle rustling."

Since Hogan wanted a grip that would ensure more distance off the tee, Longworth had him hold the club conventionally, with the left hand closer to the butt-end of the club. However, Longworth also told Hogan to do something that was unconventional: turn both hands to the right, in a clockwise direction, so that the back of the left hand and the palm of the right practically faced the

**D**uring his early playing years, bad fundamentals caused Ben Hogan to make an overly loose swing, finish in an incorrect reverse-C finish position, and hit severe hook shots.

sky. This grip was used by the early Scottish players at St. Andrews Golf Club in Scotland, since it made the ball fly low and cheat the winds blowing in from the North Sea, which borders this most famous of links courses. What Hogan was given was a truly unorthodox grip, designed to produce added distance, through lower flight and overspin.

Describing this grip in *Power Golf*, Hogan said: "Looking down on my left hand I can easily see the first three hand-knuckle joints." Any good teacher will tell you that Hogan is seeing a "strong grip." Hogan was thrilled because, among his peers, this grip made him feel like King Kong. As a result, his enthusiasm for the game grew. So much so that he lost interest in school and eventually dropped out to play the amateur circuit. However, he struggled. The reason that Hogan was drummed in tournaments week after week by the likes of Byron Nelson was that he missed the fairways and greens and made too many double-bogeys. The same strong grip that turned him into a long-drive hero was now stopping him from winning. Only Hogan failed to realize this. So he began spending hours and hours on the practice tee, making other changes to his swing, in an attempt to cure his violent hook. Ironically, had Hogan gone back to Longworth for a lesson on improving accuracy, or gotten tutoring from another pro, he would have almost certainly been advised to change his grip. But Hogan was too proud and stubborn to ask for help. Not only that, he enjoyed the challenge of trying to solve the mystery of his swing faults. Hogan was sure he would discover the swing secret that would bring him into the winner's circle, so he turned pro at age 18. This stubborn attitude of Hogan's almost cost him his career.

The more experimenting he did on the practice range, the worse he got. Instead of finding a swing that would allow him to hit the ball more accurately and get the ball into the hole in fewer shots, he dug himself deeper and deeper into a hole. He was so unsuccessful that he had to take up various jobs at country clubs in order to make ends meet.

In chapter two, I will explain, in detail, how Hogan corrected his faulty swing and finally broke through. But I first want to review the mistakes he made. These same errors in setup and swing are common among club-level players, for the simple reason that we all want to hit the ball far. In the search for distance, though, the elements of the setup and swing that help promote accurate shots are ignored. When reading about Hogan's faults in the text that follows, and looking at the accompanying artwork, determine if they match your own positions. If so, I suggest you make changes to your technique based on how Hogan dramatically changed the way he addressed the ball and swung the club.

## Hogan's Early Setup and Swing Faults

The natural instinct, for any golfer, is to swing the club with the hands. After all, the hands are the only contact your body has with the golf club. Hogan was no different than most golfers. After being taught to turn his hands to the right for more distance, he did what 99 percent of all new golfers do: turned his hands farther to the right, simply because this position gave him a sense of strength. Again, had Hogan asked Longworth or another pro for an accuracy tip, rather than a power tip, he would never have positioned his hands on the club in this way. That was not the case.

In gripping the club, Hogan held the handle almost entirely in his fingers. This hold enables you to generate faster clubhead speed, but when you take it to the extreme, as Hogan did, the tendency is to lose control of the club, regrip at the start of the downswing, and misguide the club into the ball at impact. In a good golf swing, the movement of the body must move in harmony with the movement of the club. Since the grip is the engine room of the swing, when you make a mistake holding the club, the tempo and rhythm of your swing are thrown so far out of sync that the shots you hit fly astray.

To determine if your grip is overly strong, take your normal setup position, with the bottom (sole) of the club virtually flat on the ground behind the ball, and the face of the club at right angles to a target a few yards ahead of you. Next, look down. If at least three knuckles of your left hand are clearly visible, your grip matches the one used by Hogan in his early days as an amateur and pro, when he had trouble hitting the ball accurately. To confirm what you see, have a friend face you while you are in this setup position, and look closely at your grip. He or she should also notice three knuckles and verify that the Vs formed by the thumbs and forefingers of your hands both point up at your right shoulder. If you have an exceptionally strong grip, the Vs will probably point outside your right shoulder.

I mentioned earlier that Hogan's strong finger grip caused him problems when he reached the top of the swing and started down. Hogan's regripping problem was spotted first in 1937 by Harry Cooper, a transplanted pro from England who played well enough to be inducted into golf's Hall of Fame. Cooper instructed Hogan to grip the club more tightly at the top. This tip helped Hogan make solid contact with the ball a little more consistently, but did not make a dramatic change in the accuracy of his shotmaking game. The reason it did not is because the position of Hogan's right pinky was not resting atop his left forefinger, which is the classic overlap grip position. Letting it rest between the first two fingers of the left hand is an acceptable alternative, but Hogan did not go that route either.

The overlap grip, sometimes referred to as the Vardon grip, was popularized by Harry Vardon, the supremely talented Englishman who won the 1900 U.S. Open and won the British Open a record six times, in 1896, 1898, 1899, 1903, 1911, and 1914. The Vardon grip is used by the majority of the professionals on the PGA Tour, Senior PGA Tour, and LPGA Tour. Hogan preferred this grip over the interlock grip, the next most popular hold, which is used by Jack Nicklaus. One thing was wrong, however. Because Hogan turned his hands so far to the

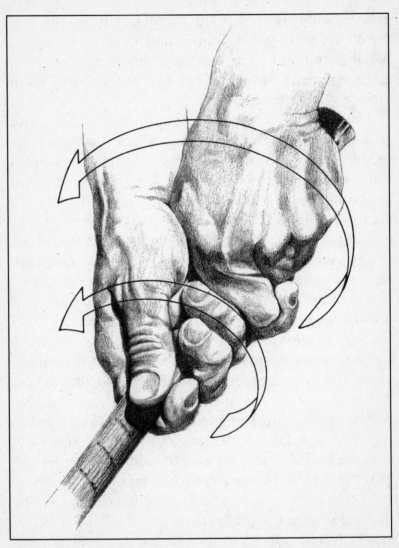

**S**witching to a very strong grip forced Hogan to hit shots that won him driving contests but cost him valuable strokes on the golf course. The reason: Many of his drives missed the fairway.

**H**ogan's faulty right pinky position prevented him from having a secure connection with the club.

right, his right pinky slipped out of the ideal position recommended by Vardon. When Hogan held the club, his right pinky was draped so loosely across the left forefinger, and at such a severe angle, that there was a loose connection between the hands and the club. This was precisely why Hogan lost control at the top of the swing, felt the need to regrip, and hit hook shots.

Another reason Hogan had trouble keeping the ball on the short grass during his early playing years was that he extended his left thumb down the side of the shaft. This "long thumb" position is not popular among expert players, largely because it causes you to overhinge the left wrist at the top, make too long a backswing, and lose control of the club on the downswing.

Hogan's extra-strong grip caused him to swing on such an exaggerated flat angle or plane that the club swung behind his body. This is not where you want the club to be. Also, Hogan's hip turn was too rotational, a fault that made the swing overly rounded, so the club swung back too far inside the target line, into an area many teachers refer to as the "point of no return."

In his former years, Hogan believed what many amateurs believe: the more you turn your hips and shoulders, the more power is created in the swing. This is not true according to Jim McLean, who is based at the Doral Golf Learning Center in Miami, Florida, and is one of *GOLF Magazine*'s top one hundred teachers in America.

"The key to the creation of power relies on the hips providing resistance to the upper body, which means their turn must be restricted," he says.

**10**

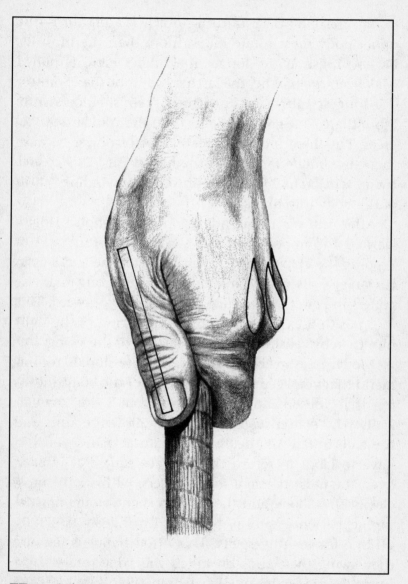

**H**ogan's overly strong left-hand grip led to swing problems, compounded by his long thumb position.

"To make a powerful turn—not just a big turn—the upper body must rotate much more than the hips. It's like a slingshot: the longer the rubber band is pulled back from the handle, the farther the stone flies. Some of the longest hitters on tour turn their shoulders little more than 70 degrees—far less than the standard 90 degrees. But these pros still create a lot of power because their hips rotate far less on the backswing. This creates rotary tension and leads to a powerful unwinding action of the body into impact."

After hitting thousands of practice shots, Hogan learned the importance of restricting hip-turn and of keeping the club in front of his body on the backswing. Hogan also discovered that he had been wrong to advise golfers in *Power Golf* to turn the right foot outward. This foot position exaggerates the coiling action of the right hip, thereby causing power to leak out of the swing.

Modern-day teachers and tour professionals recommend that you keep the club in front of the body, meaning that you should never flatten your swing dramatically. The consensus is that if you allow the arms and the club to fall well below your natural plane, you will have to labor to return the clubface square at impact. Even the most talented flat swingers, with supple muscles in their body and the time to spend hours practicing, experience slump periods, hitting shots wildly off-line for lengthy spells. This often happens because they swing their arms on much the same rotary backswing plane as the one on which their shoulders are turning, thereby moving the club drastically inside the

**H**ogan hit past his chin to encourage solid clubface-to-ball contact and a controlled power-fade shot. If your right shoulder juts outward at the start of the downswing and you come over the top like many other recreational golfers, this tip will help you hit the ball longer and much more accurately.

As soon as Hogan hit a drive and picked up the tee peg, he'd start walking to the ball while staring intently at the green and carefully planning out the ideal approach shot. This same mental discipline will give you the best opportunity to shoot the lowest possible score on a hole, and prevent you from recording the "big number."

**A**fter Hogan shifted his hips laterally toward the target, at the start of the downswing, he rotated the hips briskly in a counterclockwise direction, clearing the left hip and firing the right hip. This coordinated lower-body action allows you to return the clubface squarely to the ball at a very fast speed.

According to Sam Snead, Hogan's right-arm extension allowed him to swing the club along the target line in the hitting area, so that its face made square contact with the ball at impact. This downswing action also allowed Hogan to take very shallow divots. If you hit fat iron shots or "flyers," this tip will cure you of your problems.

**H**ogan never picked a club out of the bag until he was absolutely sure it was the right one for the job. He considered such variables as yardage, speed, and direction of wind, the firmness of the green, and the position of the flagstick. Hogan liked to land the ball in an area of the green that would leave him a level or uphill putt.

**O**nce near the green, Hogan entered a cocoon of intense concentration, working out the next shot he would play in his mind. He figured out the right technique, then envisioned the shot in his mind. For example, on chips, he imagined the ball flying in the air, landing on the green, taking a gentle hop, then rolling to the hole.

**A**fter hitting an approach, Hogan walked toward the green, determining exactly how he would play his next shot, whether it was a chip, sand shot, or putt, according to CBS golf analyst and former U.S. Open champion Ken Venturi. The same strategy will help you minimize silly mistakes that cost you added strokes.

**H**ogan was always thinking about how to get the ball in the hole in the least number of shots. Here, while waiting his turn to play, he watches a fellow competitor's ball being putted across the green. This bird's-eye view will help you determine the speed and slope of the green and sink more putts.

When hitting a pitch shot, particularly early in the round, Hogan looked intently at how the ball reacted in the air and on the ground. Hogan told Johnny Myers, one of *GOLF Magazine*'s top one hundred teachers, that this strategy gave him feedback on what he was doing right or wrong, and how the ball spun once it hit the green.

In playing a very short chip, off tightly mowed fairway grass, Hogan swung the club back on an upright angle, then sort of stabbed the club into the ground, about a half-inch behind the ball. This secret allowed him to loft the ball into the air quickly, so that it flew over the heavy fringe-grass and landed softly next to the hole.

When facing a very difficult chip, such as this short one over high fringe grass, Hogan spent extra time visualizing the shot. Next, he chose a club that allowed him to play the exact same shot he had imagined. "If club-level players followed Hogan's example, they'd shoot lower scores," says renowned instructor Rick Grayson.

**W**hen marking the ball on the green, Hogan looked closely at the
grain of the grass. A silvery sheen to the grass means the putt is
down-grain and the ball will roll faster. To adjust, make either a
shorter or slower stroke. A dull look to the grass means the putt is
against the grain, so make a longer or firmer stroke.

A fter determining the slope of the green, Hogan laid the putter down practically flat on the grass, aiming it at the breaking point between the ball and the hole. Next, he stared at that specific spot, knowing that if the ball rolled over it at the proper speed he would hit his prime target—the hole! Copy his routine.

During his heyday, Hogan was a superb putter. He putted exceptionally well in 1953 when he won all three major championships he
entered. He controlled the stroke totally with his arms and shoulders.
He also hit the ball on the upswing, contacting its top half. This secret
allows the ball to roll better and hold its line.

**A**nother reason Hogan putted so well, particularly within close range, is that he set up with his eyes directly over the ball. This position promotes a straight back-and-through stroke, which is the best action according to putting expert Dave Pelz. If you push putts, you're probably setting up with your eyes well inside the ball.

**H**ogan practiced purposefully, sometimes until sundown, a quality that set him apart from his fellow competitors. Before the round, he began practicing with a nine-iron, then hit the same shots he planned to play on the course. After the round, he spent time ironing out swing faults or perfecting a long or short shot.

target line. The player's hip turn becomes so rounded that he or she appears to be swinging inside a giant teacup. For this reason, I believe all golfers should direct their arms upward rather than around the body in the backswing, so their shoulders will turn on a slightly flatter plane. However, it is crucial that you do not confuse an upright arm swing with a straight-up arm swing, because that will cause you to lift the club abruptly skyward, producing a powerless chopping motion on the downswing.

Many average players swing the club on too flat a plane, just like Hogan once did, because they are told to "swing inside." This familiar tip can cause you to pull the club violently inside the target line during the takeaway, then farther behind you as you continue back. It's true that the club should swing slightly inside the target line at the initial stage of the backswing, but never so far behind you that the swing flattens out. If you have no idea where the club is swinging, and tend to hit score-wrecking hooks or block shots, have someone videotape your action, then review it.

As Greg Norman told me in 1997, shortly after he had started taking lessons from David Leadbetter: "The downswing is supposed to happen in reaction to the backswing, with no conscious manipulation of the hands or arms. This is much easier to accomplish if you keep the club in front of your body by making an upright swing. The upright swing feels more natural, requires less practice, and is easier to repeat."

Before telling you what you can learn from Hogan's

other mistakes, I would like to share with you three fantastic drills for correcting a flat plane. The first was shown to me by Jim Flick, the second by Jim McLean, the third by Rick Smith. I had the pleasure of working with these three world-renowned teachers during my 16-year tenure as instruction editor for *GOLF Magazine*. I also have written books with McLean and Smith.

To train yourself to swing the clubhead consistently on a more upright plane, Flick recommends that you stand close enough to a wall that the head of an old club brushes against it. Start with your hands just above waist height. Next, swing the arms and hands around and up, then down, with the clubhead staying against the wall. Do this drill slowly so you feel the correct physical motion and incorporate it into your golf swing.

To correct the same overly flat swing-plane problem as Hogan's, McLean suggests that you first take your normal address with a driver. Next, have a friend stand behind you, holding a club so its shaft is horizontal to the ground and parallel to your body-line. Swing back to the halfway point, with the goal to keep the shaft of your club slightly outside the other club.

Smith recommends that you have a friend squat behind you, holding a clubshaft directly above your body-line. Swing the club back to waist height, trying to keep the shaft parallel to the ground and above the other shaft, with the toe of the clubhead pointing at the sky.

Another factor that made Hogan a slow starter was the length of his backswing. It was very long and very loose, partly because of his faulty grip and partly because he had an obsession with length off the tee. Distance is important because, logically, the farther you hit the drive, the shorter the second shot. The shorter the second shot, the more lofted the club required. Logically, too, lofted clubs are easier to hit and control. Further, short irons hit the ball higher, so you can stop the ball more quickly next to the hole. The trouble is that long drives do more harm than good if they land in the rough or woods, rather than the fairway. Later in his career, when Hogan took the time to analyze his game, he realized this basic truth about golf and, as a result, shortened his swing.

Whenever the swing is long, the wrists tend to collapse at the top. When the wrists overhinge, the natural thing to do is to throw the club at the ball with the hands, rather than start the downswing with the lower body. There is no way you can recover after releasing the hands and wrists too early on the downswing, or "casting" the club. Hogan had superior eye-hand coordination and tremendous feel in his hands, so he could usually bail out and hit fairly decent shots. But, on two or three holes per round, he hooked the ball so severely that he often lost vital strokes to par. On the professional golf tour, or when playing competitively at your home course, you can not afford such mistakes. To position yourself to hit on-target approach shots into greens and shoot the best possible score, you must keep the ball in play.

Once Hogan began trying to alleviate his hook by experimenting on the practice tee with different move-

15

**H**ogan's "long" left thumb forced his left wrist to hinge too much at the top and promoted an overly long backswing.

ments such as triggering the downswing with his hips, the problem got worse. It's true that if you make a lateral lower-body shift on the downswing, you will prevent the hands and arms from shutting the clubface at impact and imparting severe right-to-left hook-spin on the ball. However, the young Hogan did not shift his hips laterally toward the target. Rather, he rotated them briskly in a counterclockwise direction at the split second he reached the top of his swing. This downswing trigger caused Hogan to hit more severe hook shots, because when you clear the hips before shifting them laterally, you encourage the hands and arms to release more freely and close the clubface in the hitting area. Hogan must have felt this, but he failed to realize the harm being done because he believed that when you rotate the left hip to the left to trigger the downswing action, it gives the hands and arms a head start.

"You do not want the hands and arms to get a running start," says teaching guru Phil Ritson.

"To generate power, they must lag behind. The essence of the golf swing is to keep the club away from the ball as long as possible, so that you preserve power. The only time you unleash the club powerfully is in the hitting area."

Had Hogan done what David Duval and Annika Sorenstam do today—let their head rotate toward the target before impact—he would have promoted a lateral shift. But he did not. Hogan kept his head so locked in position that too much weight remained on his right foot through impact and, in turn, this fault caused him

**17**

to release his right arm, right hand, and the club prematurely, in an exaggerated fashion.

When you hold the club like Hogan did, swing back on an overly flat plane, and exaggerate the clearing action of the hips on the downswing, while keeping the head locked in position, it follows that the releasing action of the arms and hands will be faulty. In Hogan's case, the counterclockwise rotation of his right hand and forearm was so fast that he could do very little to prevent shutting the clubface at impact.

In analyzing Hogan's original, flawed power-golf swing, I think one of the key reasons his release was so quick is that he felt the club behind him, well inside the target line. To Hogan, a quick downswing tempo was a necessity. Seemingly, he thought that only by speeding up the action of his hands and arms could he return the club squarely to the ball. Of course, Hogan managed to do that on occasion during his early years but, more often than not, he mistimed the swing and was plagued by bad shots that led to high scores. In time, Hogan would learn that tempo is maybe the single most important element of the swing.

The key is to find the correct tempo for you, as I learned from Seve Ballesteros when collaborating with him on the book *Natural Golf*, and when I played a round of golf with him in 1986 at the LaManga Club in Spain. You must determine the maximum speed at which you can swing and still remain in total command of your body and the club. Some very fine players swing fast, while others swing comparatively more slowly. Nev-

**R**estraining natural head movement and employing an exaggerated right arm and hand release-action was one of the chief reasons Hogan suffered from severe hook problems in his early years as a professional.

ertheless, every top-notch PGA Tour professional swings with the tempo—his ideal tempo—that allows him repeatedly to meet the back of the ball with the center of the clubface squarely aligned to the target and traveling at speed.

The thought of correct tempo should always be in the back of your mind as you work on your swing mechanics because poor tempo frequently nullifies even the best mechanics. However, the comforting fact here is that developing good tempo becomes a lot easier when you have good mechanics.

In contrast, faulty mechanics create bad tempo, simply because they make the swinging action so anatomically awkward and stressful. The root of the problem usually lies in the player's setup. For example, a faulty grip like Hogan's early hold can result in poor positions on the backswing and too fast a tempo on the downswing. The player who grips too loosely tends to swing the club solely with his hands, and thus quicken his tempo coming down in a vain search for power. Other setup mistakes can cause similar problems, so whenever you sense your tempo is out of sync always check your preswing fundamentals first.

Work on determining your own ideal tempo by experimenting with the speed or pace of your swing components until you find the combination that permits full control, time and again, over your body and the golf club. Keeping your body as free of tension as possible, swing faster and faster until you stop making solid contact and/or your shots start flying wildly. Then throttle back to a swing speed that enables you, once again, to produce powerful, well-directed shots. Then feel and mentally record that perfect personal tempo. Thereafter, keep practicing at your pace until eventually it becomes second nature.

When you consider that Hogan won nine major titles, is only one of four men to win the Masters, U.S. Open, PGA, and British Open championships (the others being Gene Sarazen, Gary Player, and Jack Nicklaus), and, along with Bobby Jones and Willie Anderson, is one of only three men to have won four U.S. Opens, it's hard to believe he ever played the game any way but spectacularly. But he did go through very poor stretches of play. Hogan was so unhappy that during 1930, his debut year as a pro, he quit before the finish of the first two pro tournaments he entered. What's worse, 10 long years went by before he won his first golf tournament, and 16 before he won his first major championship.

Because Hogan struggled to search for a swing that repeated itself under pressure, weekend golfers could relate to him. What's more, once they saw that he climbed from virtual obscurity to the top of the golfing world, they sensed he had learned something no other golfer had before him. Did Hogan know the secret to the swing? That was the question all golfers were asking.

Hogan first let on that he had a secret in 1947, but it was never revealed until years later. Up until that time, pros and amateurs alike tried to guess just what was Hogan's secret. Others brushed Hogan's claim off as some sort of psyche-out maneuver. One pro even called

Hogan a liar. Since Hogan won eight major championships after announcing he had a secret, three in 1953 alone, one can imagine how the golfing public was champing at the bit to find out what made Hogan's technique tick. Professionals Gene Sarazen and Mike Turnesa came closest to guessing that Hogan's secret had something to do with fanning the clubface wide open on the backswing. How good was this secret? Well, this is what Cary Middlecoff had to say in the book *The Golf Swing*:

> I have had many swing secrets, many of which I briefly thought were so valuable that I would keep them strictly to myself until I had won all the tournaments and money I wanted to. But none ever impressed me sufficiently or worked for a long enough time period to tempt me to announce now I really got it. Hogan's did.

Hogan's so-called secret was revealed in a 1955 *Life* magazine cover story, showing photographs of his secret setup and swing positions. That year Middlecoff won the Masters. Hogan finished second. The following year Middlecoff won the U.S. Open. Hogan finished runner-up.

Let's now take a closer look at Hogan's secrets, the misnomers about his technique, and the "lost fundamentals"—those magical setup and swing keys he never shared with anyone.

# 2

## Corrective Measures

•

The setup and swing secrets Hogan
talked about, and those that were never
shared before now, can help you become
a more skillful wood and iron player

---

Those of you who play the game well likely hit a controlled shot of some kind, be it a power-fade like Hogan, or a controlled draw like Tiger Woods and David Duval.

The draw is a much more difficult shot than the power-fade to hit and control consistently, which is why most pros, including Jack Nicklaus, prefer to work their ball from left to right as Hogan did.

If you are a middle to high handicap player, it is likely that you move the ball from left to right, only on such a severe flight pattern that your most common good shot is probably a controlled slice, at least when your tempo and timing is good. Don't worry if that's the case. By making some simple changes to your setup and swing, and sacrificing some playing time for practice time, you can become a more consistent shotmaker.

There are various reasons why golfers slice. Ironically, nearly every time I tee up with players who slice shots, I notice that the majority employ a very strong, so-called hooker's grip, just like Hogan's early hold. The only reason Hogan hit hook shots rather than slices when using such a faulty grip was that his hand action and hip rotation was much more lively than the average golfer's. An extra-strong grip will give you a false sense of security and probably cause you to swing the club on an exaggerated inside-out path. Consequently, you will also hit the ball off-line.

One of the secrets Hogan revealed in the 1955 *Life* article was a change to a "weak" grip. In 1940, golf pro and friend Henry Picard suggested Hogan employ this type hold, by moving his hands toward the target when he gripped the club. Hogan listened to Picard's tip, but still fought an occasional hook problem for a while after the lesson because of his exceptionally fast hip and hand action.

To better understand Hogan's secret, you need to appreciate Hogan's thinking process at the time. In early 1946, he tried all the conventional ways of curing an agonizing hook, such as opening the stance. They all worked, but Hogan was disappointed because, in the process, he lost distance. He became so distraught that he decided to spend some time at home in Fort Worth and meditate on the golf swing without picking up a club. One night while lying in bed and thinking about

**H**ogan's "new" fundamentals and added muscular strength enabled him to make a more powerful on-balance swing. Letting part of his left hand protrude over the edge of the grip was a secret he never shared.

technique, Hogan visualized the old Scottish pros. Almost immediately the solution to his shotmaking problem came to him.

Hogan visualized himself setting up to the ball just like the old pros, except he would change his grip. He moved his left hand to the left so that the thumb was almost directly on top of the shaft. During the backswing, he would let his hands roll gradually to the right, or "pronate," so that at the top the back of the left hand faced almost straight up and the back of the right hand almost straight down. He also cupped his left wrist gradually backward and inward on the backswing. In theory, Hogan figured these changes would cause the face of the club to open on the backswing. And, on the way down, the face of the club would gradually close until it returned to a slightly open position at impact.

The next morning Hogan arrived on the practice tee, anxious to put his theory to the test. He hit balls for eight hours, and for all that time he hit powerful shots that flew straight off the clubface, faded slightly at the end, and sat down quickly.

During the next week Hogan hit the ball even better, so he decided to see if this swing could perform under pressure. He went to Chicago for George May's double tournament. He proved his new swing worked by winning both events.

"No matter how much wrist I put into the downswing, no matter how hard I swung or how hard I tried to roll into and through the ball, the face of the club could not close fast enough to become absolutely square at the moment of impact," said Hogan in *Life* magazine. "The result was that lovely, long-fading ball which is a highly effective weapon on the golf course."

What made this story so incredible was at the end of it Hogan discouraged readers from trying his technique. "I doubt it will be worth a doggone to the weekend duffer and it will ruin a bad golfer," said Hogan. Many golfers felt cheated by this comment of Hogan's. But I think he was just covering himself. The truth is, the story was not a con job. Actually Hogan provided golfers with some valuable information, which was possibly all he knew at the time.

Some critics go so far as to say that Hogan held some of his information back because he planned to include other instructional tips in *Five Lessons*. And there is some truth to that. Hogan did share more secrets for hitting a controlled power-fade shot in his second instruction book. The trouble is, he failed to mention some of the most crucial technical mechanics important to his methods of setting up to the ball and swinging the club. Furthermore, illustrations contradicted what he said in the text.

## The New Fundamentals

One of the secrets Hogan shared with readers in *Five Lessons* was his new right-foot position at address. Hogan recommended that the golfer set up with the right foot perpendicular to the target line to turn precisely the right amount. Apparently, Hogan had learned through trial and error that this position restricted the turning action of his right hip and helped build resistance between the upper and lower body. This torque, Hogan discovered, yields added clubhead speed and power. (As a matter of note, in *Power Golf* Hogan recommended that both feet point outward, and in *Life* he did not discuss this element of the setup, seemingly because he thought it was unimportant.)

This perpendicular right-foot position also prevents the head and body from swaying on the backswing. Additionally, it discourages you from swinging the club on an overly flat plane. So, Hogan had discovered a true secret to hitting powerfully accurate shots.

Another of Hogan's tips involved the grip. Hogan recommended a weak grip, telling players to let the club lie diagonally across the top joint of the forefinger and under the muscular pad of the left hand. Hogan wanted the player to let the club lay straight across the top joint of the four fingers and below the palm of the right hand. This was not new. Vardon had told golfers that this was one of his secrets long ago. What was new? Hogan recommended that the V of the left hand point up at the player's right eye and the V of the right hand point up at his or her chin. This was a complete turnaround for Hogan, who had long employed a strong grip. In *Life* he had recommended moving the hands to the left, but now he had taken it to the extreme. Golfing great Byron Nelson and other experts believed this change prevented Hogan from closing the clubface at the top of the swing and at impact, thereby stopping his hook problem. Teaching guru David Leadbetter agrees that Hogan's weak right-hand grip ultimately prevented the toe of the clubhead from passing its heel and hitting a hook.

Obviously, because Hogan made such a dramatic change to his grip, he had discovered just what a critical bearing the hold has on the type of swing you put on the ball. The old extra-strong grip encouraged him to swing the club back well inside the target line with his hands. Hogan's new weak grip allowed him to better control the path and plane of the club. One more thing: When you weaken the grip, it is far easier to keep the left arm extended on the backswing, and this was something Hogan did all of the time. Being a short man, this extended left arm was a particularly vital link to power. You must understand that when the left arm is allowed to be an extension of the golf club's shaft, at address and during the motion, the arc of the swing is maximized. This was one chief reason why Hogan hit the ball longer than taller men who let their left arm bend slightly on the backswing.

"Hogan was a detail man, which explains why he recommended practicing holding the club with a weak grip for one-half hour each day," said Desmond Tolhurst, a former instruction editor of *GOLF Magazine*. "Hogan learned the hard way that the grip was the principal feature of the setup, as evidenced by the opening sentence in the first chapter of *Five Lessons*: "Good golf begins with a good grip.'"

To determine if you are holding the club correctly, have a friend try to pull the club out of your hands. If your friend feels a slight bit of resistance as he or she slides the grip out of your hands, your grip is just fine. If

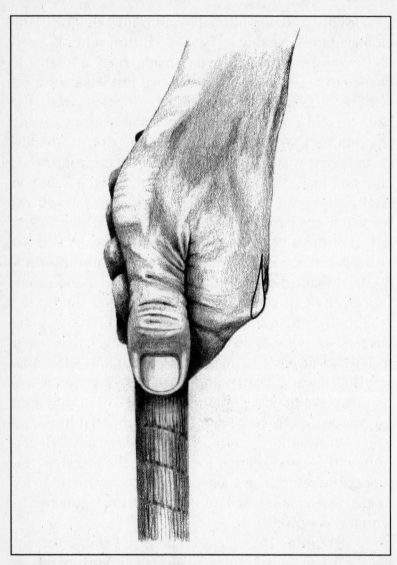

**H**ogan's weak, two-knuckle left-hand grip (above), and weak right-hand grip (right) promoted an open clubface position at impact and a controlled power-fade shot.

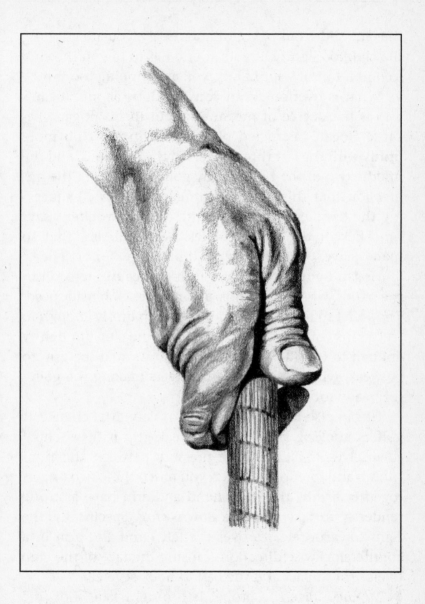

the club slides out of your hands easily, you are gripping the club too lightly. If your friend has to tug on the club to pull it out of your hands, you are gripping too firmly.

What is overlooked in conversations about Hogan's grip is the degree of pressure he put in his fingers. Because Hogan instructed players to grip the club more firmly with the last three fingers of the left hand, and the middle two of the right, many golfers are under the impression that this master shotmaker advocated squeezing the handle of the club hard. "It's no wonder," says Jim Flick of the Nicklaus-Flick Golf Schools, "that so many players grip the club as if preparing for violence."

Hogan figured out that a firm grip causes tension in the hands, wrists, and arms, and reduces clubhead speed. The secret to reducing tension is to grip firmly enough to feel a sense of security when holding the club but lightly enough to feel the clubhead. Hogan wanted the grip to be weak, with pressure in the fingers making the golfer feel ready for action.

Hogan also learned that there is very little chance of golfers hooking shots using a weak grip if they school themselves to lighten the pressure between the right thumb and forefinger. When you pinch these two fingers together firmly, the right hand and arm have a strong tendency to take over the downswing. Specifically, the right forearm releases over the left hand and arm in a counterclockwise direction, causing the face of the club to close at impact and the ball to hook severely.

To encourage the proper left-to-right fade shot, the left side must take control. You must hold onto the club more tightly with only the last three fingers of the left hand and the middle two of the right, as per Hogan's instructions, but the rest of the fingers must be relaxed on the club, especially those in the right hand. You want to feel that during the swing the right hand goes along for the ride. Coming into impact, the right forearm should also be behind the left, not outside it, which is common to golfers who come over the top. When releasing the club, the right elbow should be near the right hip and ahead of the right forearm. Hogan compared the proper movement of the right arm and hand to that made by a baseball infielder when he throws to first base.

The idea, at this point in the book, is to examine Hogan's swing in sequence, examining his address first, then analyzing his backswing technique, and finally looking at what was good and what was bad about his advice on the downswing. So, it's better to hold back on any further discussions about the releasing action and focus first on the start of the action.

Hogan recommended that players move the club back and forth, or "waggle it." First, move the club away from the target for a short distance to get accustomed to the path it will take on the backswing; second, move it back square to the ball to rehearse the into-impact attack-track. According to swing aficionados, Hogan added the waggle to his swing in 1932 after noting how Johnny Revolta geared his swing for short shots.

The waggle requires that the player hinge the wrists dramatically. This idiosyncratic feature of Hogan's swing is excellent for promoting feel for the clubhead, but it has its dangers if exaggerated. If you hinge the wrists immediately in the takeaway, you will probably pick up the club on an overly steep angle, hit down sharply with an open clubface, and slice the ball. Taking this danger into account, be sure to experiment with the waggle in practice before trying it during play on the course.

As for the relationship between the address and the actual swing, Hogan recommended in *Five Lessons* that golfers become aware of the angle on which they swing the club upward and downward by imagining the swing plane as a pane of glass. At address, Hogan pictured the plane tilting from his shoulders down to the ball. When Hogan's arms approached hip level on the backswing, they moved parallel with the plane and remained parallel with the plane (just below the glass) to the top of the backswing. On the downswing, Hogan's club fell into a shallower plane once he turned his hips back to the left.

Taller players, who set their hands relatively high at address, stand close to the ball, and use clubs that feature a more upright lie, automatically swing on a steeper plane. Short players, who set up to the ball with their hands lower, stand farther from the ball, and use clubs featuring a flatter lie, normally swing the club on a flatter plane. Hogan believed that if the arms and the club swung well below a player's established plane, he or she was directing the club along an overly flat plane. If the arms and club rise above the player's natural plane, the swing is too upright.

Hogan's image of the plane definitely makes the golfer aware of the angle on which he swings the club, both on the backswing and the through swing. Some teachers and tour professionals argue that this awareness helps a player concentrate on where the club is at all times. So if the player makes a mistake while swinging, he or she can correct it before the crucial point of impact, or at least pinpoint the error and learn from it. Others argue that this obsession with the plane disturbs the free-flowing continuity of the swing. It is just one more thing to think about. They believe that if you are fitted with the proper equipment and set up to the ball correctly for your height, you will most likely swing the club on the correct angle without thinking about anything.

You can use video to see if you are swinging too upright or flat. In all fairness to Hogan, his image was probably more helpful at the time he wrote the book because teachers could not videotape a student's swing. Besides, there were not as many teachers giving lessons. Consequently, students had to depend on feel. Now, almost all instructors use video. Still, Hogan's pane-of-glass image was a lasting contribution to golf instruction because he made golfers aware of the club's position. Nowhere is this more important than on the backswing, since how you swing back has a great influence on how you swing through.

When Hogan swung the club back to the top, he bent his left wrist inward, so that an indentation or "cup" was created by the back of the left wrist and the back of the left hand. This innovative move of Hogan's opened the clubface, so he could swing down aggressively and not fear hooking.

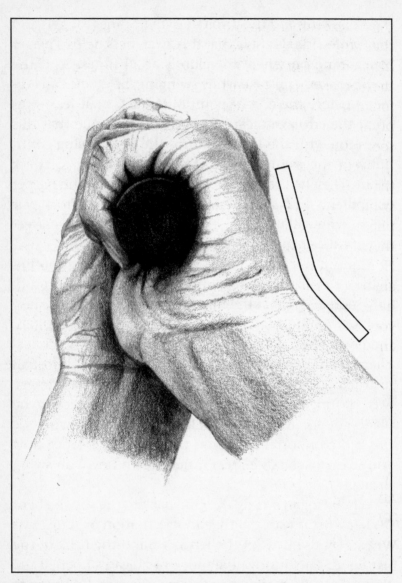

**T**he "cup" in Hogan's left wrist protected him from hitting severe hook shots.

What even the keenest golfers do not appreciate is that when Hogan played his best golf, he occasionally hit a controlled draw. He accomplished this by keeping the back of his left wrist "flat" (lined up with the left forearm) on the backswing. On the downswing, he simply altered his hip action, clearing his left hip a trifle sooner and faster.

What surprised me most when reading *Five Lessons* is that Hogan fails to mention four setup keys, one backswing key, and one very critical downswing key. The rare photographs I possess show him in these positions. I call these secrets Hogan's "Lost Fundamentals." Maybe Hogan hid these from us and wanted golfers to find the answer to the swing "in the dirt"—his expression for hard, honest practice. In any case, I will show these to you, because these are the true secrets to curing the slice and learning to hit a Hogan-like power-fade shot.

## The Lost Fundamentals: The Secrets That Hogan Never Shared

## THE ADDRESS

ADDRESS KEY NUMBER ONE:
"CLOSE" YOUR STANCE

When hitting the driver and most other clubs, Hogan set his feet down in a "closed" position, meaning that his right foot was a few inches farther away from the target line than his left foot. This address position offset the tendency he had to swing the club back outside the target line during the backswing, owing to his very weak grip. The slightly closed stance position allowed Hogan to swing the club back along the target line, at the earliest stage of the takeaway, then slightly inside as he swung further back. If you use a grip like Hogan's, match his right foot position. If, on the other hand, you hold the club with a neutral grip, with the Vs formed by your thumbs and forefingers pointing up midway between your chin and right shoulder, you should set up square with your feet equidistant from the target line. Don't worry, you can still hit a fade from this stance by holding on slightly more firmly with the left hand through the impact zone. This firm hand action will allow you to come into impact with the clubface slightly open, provided you don't "strangle" the handle.

ADDRESS KEY NUMBER TWO:
TAKE AN EXTRA-WIDE STANCE

When setting up to drive the ball, spread your feet six inches wider than the width of your shoulders. This super-wide stance promotes a long takeaway action of the club and helps create a wide swing arc. Surprisingly, Hogan never mentioned this vital setup key in *Five Lessons*. He simply explained that in setting up to a five-iron he set his feet shoulder width apart, then, as the clubs increased in length, progressively widened his stance. However, looking at photographs of Hogan addressing the ball to play a five-iron, you can see he spread his feet a couple of inches farther apart than the

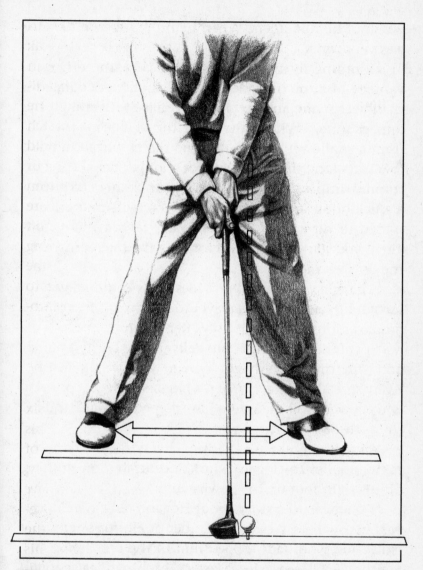

**H**ogan's "lost fundamentals" at address included an exceptionally wide closed stance and a hands-behind-the-ball position.

width of his shoulders. When he hit a driver, his stance was very wide.

According to instructor Jim McLean, "the other advantage of an extra-wide stance is that it encourages a shallower swing and an elongated flat-spot through the impact-zone." When you bring the club into the ball from a shallower angle, and keep the clubhead moving low and along the target line for a longer period of time through impact, like Hogan did, your chances of hitting a duck-hook are slim to none. You will be perfectly poised to hit a power-fade, Hogan's favorite shot, provided you start shifting and rotating the hips early on in the downswing.

"The wide stance also provides a low center of gravity for stability and allows a player to 'pump' his feet off the ground more powerfully," says Ken Venturi.

"If you had one chance to deliver your hardest punch and win the heavyweight crown, you would instinctively spread your feet. When a baseball slugger connects with power, it's because he has stepped forward and hit from a broad base."

Venturi's comment on using lively foot action certainly applies to Hogan, who concentrated on pushing off his right foot on the downswing.

"I once heard a story about Hogan being asked to reveal his swing secret to a member of Florida's Seminole Golf Club who had stopped him in the bar," said Gary Smith, *GOLF Magazine* Master Teaching Professional. "Surprisingly Hogan obliged, telling the player to concentrate on rolling his weight onto the inside of his right foot on the downswing, with the right knee kicking inward and the left hip rotating rapidly in a counterclockwise direction."

ADDRESS KEY NUMBER THREE:
GRIP THE VERY END OF THE CLUB'S HANDLE

At most golf schools and country clubs, individuals are told to choke down on the club slightly, since this theoretically enhances one's control. I have a problem with this advice, unless you want to play a fancy hands-wrists shot from the fairway or a short feel-shot from around the green. But, even then, you run the risk of swinging the club away from the correct path and plane and mishitting the shot. The handle of a club is tapered, so the more you grip down, the thinner it becomes. Even if you grip down only an inch, for example, on the handle of a driver, you are not able to get as firm a hold on the club. Inevitably, the hands and wrists come into play, preventing the body's big muscles from taking control of the swing. As a result, you lose power.

Hogan was smart enough to realize that by gripping the club high on the handle, the thickness of the grip would give him a firmer sense of security and control. By gripping this way, you will feel more connected to the club and be better able to sense a oneness between the left arm and the clubshaft. Since the left side controls the swing, this is a major plus-factor. Make no mistake, it was one of Hogan's secrets to hitting accurate shots. Gripping higher on the club also gave him a bigger radius and wider arc of swing, thereby increasing his power potential.

ADDRESS KEY NUMBER FOUR:
SET UP WITH YOUR HANDS SLIGHTLY
BEHIND THE BALL

Many of today's teachers tell students to line their hands either slightly ahead of the ball or even with the ball. Hogan tried both of these setup positions but soon discovered they didn't work well. The hands-ahead position usually promotes an overly steep swing and a sharply angled downswing hit. The in-line setup works better, but it still does not promote as long a takeaway action as the hands-behind-the-ball address position.

When setting up the ball to hit a driver, fairway wood, medium iron, or long iron, Hogan set his hands a couple of inches behind the ball. Why Hogan failed to mention this very critical technical element in *Five Lessons* is beyond me, because it promotes a one-piece takeaway action of the arms, hands, and shoulders. This setup position also discourages any faulty wrist-break at the initial stage of the takeaway. Consequently, you are much more apt to swing the club on a wide arc and, as a result, make a bigger turn of the body and create more power in the swing. Further, as Lee Trevino told me, "a hands-behind-the-ball setup position allows the golfer to hit the fade more easily, especially if he or she plays the ball relatively forward in the stance."

Hogan's hands-back position also enabled him to contact the ball powerfully on the upswing, giving him little chance of hooking shots.

## THE BACKSWING

HOGAN'S NUMBER ONE BACKSWING KEY:
SHORTEN THE SWING

Over and over, in instruction books and magazine articles, golfers are told to swing the club back to the parallel position, meaning that at the top of the swing the clubshaft should be parallel to the target line. This has been considered the classic position for a very long time. Many teachers and tour pros still believe this at-the-top position gives the golfer the best chance of delivering the club squarely to the ball at impact.

Through trial and error, Hogan discovered that a shorter, three-quarter length swing works even better. One change to his grip helped Hogan employ this shorter swing. He pulled his left thumb up about a half inch, into what instructors call a "short thumb" position, and pointed it straight down the club's handle.

The majority of PGA Tour pros, such as Tiger Woods, Davis Love, and Greg Norman, agree with the short-swing philosophy because they believe it helps preserve power. As Hogan and other pros discovered over the years, when you try to swing the club back to the parallel position, the tendency is to swing past that point, with the wrists overhinging. When both wrists collapse dramatically at the top, you tend to start the downswing with the hands and throw the club at the ball. To promote a square club-to-ball impact position and added clubhead speed, you must start the downswing with the lower body and let the hands lag behind.

**H**ogan's "short" left thumb position (above) promoted a more compact swing (right).

## THE DOWNSWING

HOGAN'S NUMBER ONE DOWNSWING KEY:
SHIFT THE HIPS LATERALLY TOWARD
THE TARGET

When teachers and tour pros are asked about Hogan's secret, they often credit hip action as the key to his superior swing technique. The majority say this because that's what they observed when they watched Hogan play, or because they know he put great emphasis on the importance of hip action in *Five Lessons*.

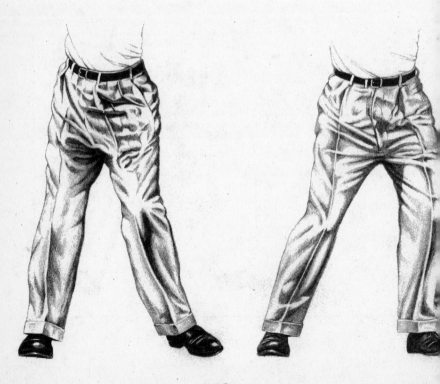

When you realize that the swing takes less than two seconds, with the downward half of the action taking approximately one-fifth of a second, I think you will agree that it is very difficult to see exactly what movements of the body and club are being made. For this reason, I take what observers say about Hogan's swing with a grain of salt.

As far as what Hogan mentions in *Five Lessons*, yes, he did explain his hip action in detail. All the same, he left out the most important point: that he shifted his hips laterally toward the target before rotating them to the

**H**ere, you can clearly see how Hogan moves from a turned position of the hips on the backswing (left), to a square position at the start of the downswing (center), to a cleared position through impact (right).

left, in a counterclockwise direction—a move Dick Harmon, one of the game's best teachers, believes discourages the clubface from closing at impact.

"Golfers who have read Hogan's advice to clear the hips as fast as possible on the downswing, as a way of generating power, have been thrown way off course," says Johnny Myers, one of *GOLF Magazine*'s top one hundred teachers in America. "They spin their hips around so abruptly that they get way out ahead of the ball and mishit the shot. The slow hand-arm-club releasers block the ball, while the fast releasers hook the ball."

By shifting his hips laterally before clearing them, Hogan gave himself ample time to stay centered in the sit-down position (knees bowed outward slightly) and wait for the club. During the lateral shift action, Hogan's knees stayed parallel to the target line, which encouraged him to keep the club moving along the proper path. Once he pushed off his right foot, he delivered the club more powerfully into impact with its face open slightly. The resulting shot flew far and straight before tailing off to the right a few degrees.

# 3

## Up Close and Personal

•

Forming a clear mental picture of
Hogan's revamped swing—the one that
made him a golfing great—will help you
hit more solid, controlled shots

L overs of culture feel very fortunate when they see
paintings, sheet music, sculptures, buildings, and
other beautiful reminders of times long ago, knowing
that great care went into preserving these masterpieces.

Lovers of golf feel very fortunate when they see rare
photographs of Ben Hogan, golf's immortal icon.
Hogan's name is eternally linked to the game he loved
and played ingeniously. He is to golf what Mozart is to
classical music, what Einstein is to science, what Ali is to
boxing.

The photographic swing sequence presented in this
chapter was shot by the late Chuck Brenkus while he was
covering his Southern California golf beat. Hogan, who
did not talk much to anyone—even his caddy got just a

basic hello and good-bye—befriended Brenkus, a fine player in his own right. Brenkus told me that Hogan had wanted to verify that he was limiting the turn of his hips, so as to produce power-generating torque between the upper and lower body, and employing a more con-trolled three-quarter swing, with his wrists firm at the top. The deal was that Brenkus could shoot the pho-tographs provided Hogan was allowed to scrutinize them. Of course, Brenkus agreed to the arrangement. Be-ing able to help golf's all-time best ball-striker and, at the same time, add this wonderful sequence to his library, was a good reciprocal arrangement.

When the idea for this book came to mind, I con-tacted Isolde Knudson-Brenkus, wife of the late photog-rapher, who had inherited the photographs as part of his estate. Thankfully, she happily agreed to allow Harper-Collins publishers to showcase these wonderful pho-tographs for the benefit of the millions of golfers who idolize Hogan but had never had the opportunity to see him in action.

The moment I looked at these photographs, I thought how determined Hogan must have been to have hit balls day in and day out in his desire to turn a faulty swing into something so fantastic. Since Hogan was blessed with more determination than raw talent, his en-ergy for practice and quest for perfection were inex-haustible. No matter how well he played, he was never satisfied. Hogan was such a perfectionist that he once dreamed he scored seventeen aces during a round, but woke up mad and sweaty, upset about the one he missed.

Since the early 1950s, professional and amateur players have been obsessed with how Hogan consistently hit a controlled power-fade shot.

Hogan is truly an inspiration to golfers around the world who struggle to find a swing that is easy to repeat. He proved to aspiring golfers that the game can be learned through trial and error combined with hard work and willpower.

"The apparent line of reasoning is that Hogan worked and thought his way up from a not-very-good golfer to the greatest in the world, so it was only logical that he would know how a golf swing is transformed from bad to good," said Cary Middlecoff in *The Golf Swing*. "In short, those who aspire to greater things in golf— whether it be to break 100 for the first time or win the club championship—tend to feel that they have something in common with Hogan. They see in him reason for trying and hoping."

Hogan's action is about as good as that of the technically perfect robots they use to test golf clubs at the United States Golf Association and at manufacturing plants owned by the likes of Callaway and Titleist. In fact, in 1963 a team of scientists and tour players made an in-depth study of the technical elements involved in hitting a golf ball. While collecting data, they devised a "model" representing the perfect golf swing. The swing that most nearly measured up to the model's representation of perfection belonged to Hogan. So, make no mistake, it is the swing to copy.

Unlike the power hitters of today, who are built like tanks, Hogan was an average-size man—5 feet 9 inches tall, 130 pounds—and not very muscular. The fact that he hit the ball so solidly and accurately, particularly in

1953 when the swing secrets he discovered allowed his game to peak at unparalleled levels, made the average golfer sit up and listen.

I have already pointed out that before Hogan's *Life* article was launched on the newsstands, top pros tried to guess Hogan's secret. The curiosity has never stopped. In March 1994, for example, long after Hogan had put his clubs away and written *Five Lessons*, *Golf Digest* ran a cover story entitled "Ben Hogan's Secret: Did He Really Tell Us Everything?" that turned out to be a blockbuster. The cover was of a gatefold style. When I opened it, there were quotes from experts on what they believed Hogan's secret was.

Ken Venturi: "It was psychological."

Cary Middlecoff: "It was the way he stuck his right elbow into his stomach."

Jack Burke Jr.: "It was the way he used his right hand."

Dick Harmon: "It was his strong lateral move on the downswing."

Gardner Dickinson: "It was his ball and hand position."

Bob Toski: "It was the way he stabilized the force of the blow with his left arm and hand."

Johnny Miller: "It was the way he buckled his left wrist."

Byron Nelson: "It was his left-hand grip."

Chuck Cook: "It was the stiffer shafts in his clubs."

After including these opinions, this line was run next: "Now, turn to page 52 for The Real Secret."

On turning to page 52, the reader was drawn into the

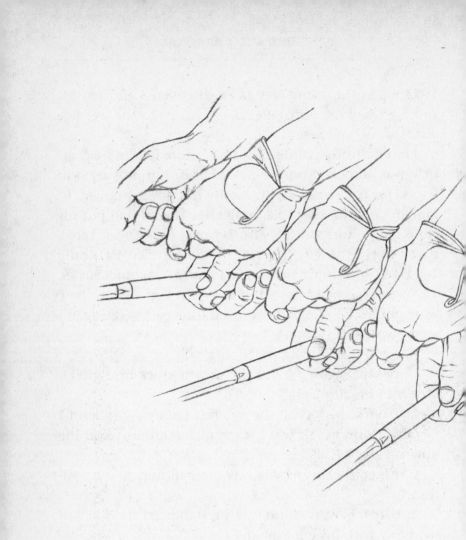

NBC golf commentator Johnny Miller, one of the most talented and knowledgeable players in the world, believes Hogan's secret was a buckled left wrist position at impact. There is no doubt that this is a critical element in hitting a power-fade shot, a fact Hogan pointed out in his book, *Five Lessons*.

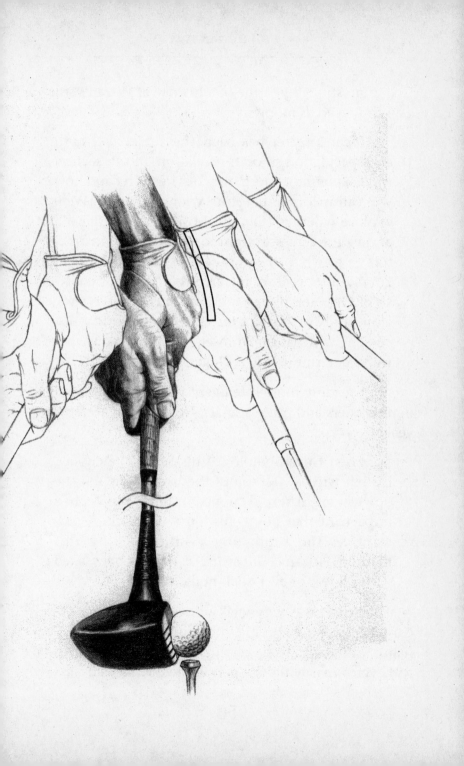

Hogan mystique by virtue of a history of Hogan's secret. The copy read as follows:

> Hogan's secret has been the subject of myth and speculation since its revelation. In this section we'll explain the mechanics of The Secret and how you can incorporate it into your own game. We'll explore whether Hogan told his Secret, after all, and venture guesses from top players and instructors as to what Hogan may have kept to himself. Finally, after years of research that included analysis of films and photographs, extensive interviews, close study of Hogan's published works and a discussion with Hogan himself, we'll tell you what we've determined to be Hogan's real secret.

After reading more intelligent guesses from other expert teachers and professionals, Hogan's real secret is revealed.

> When Hogan employed his Secret, he cupped his left wrist at the top of the backswing. On the downswing, it stayed cupped until he approached impact. At that point, his left wrist buckled outward in the supinating position. Using this method, Hogan could swing as hard as he wanted with no fear of ever duck-hooking the ball.

The article was very well written by technical editor Guy Yokum, and extremely informative, too, which explains why it was so successful. To be frank, though, the real secret involving the cupped left wrist had already been mentioned in Hogan's previous writings. However, it was smart of golf's number one publication to run this story because today's new golfers are too young to have read the *Life* article, while others have never heard of *Five Lessons*.

Today's golfers are still fascinated by Hogan, a man who was so reclusive he rarely made public appearances, distrusted the press, and was all business on the course. Up until now golfers have gained some satisfaction by purchasing Hogan's *Five Lessons* and studying it carefully to find a tip that will help them improve. The problem is that many of these enthusiasts who are anxious to improve become frustrated because the book contains no photographs of Hogan's supreme swing action. It features only black-and-white illustrations. Moreover, they are not presented in a sequential form, so the golfer gets no feel for the start-to-finish flow of Hogan's swing.

Here, you will be able to discover, through words and pictures, exactly how Hogan's power-fade swing operated, from the static address position to the backswing to the moment of impact and beyond. The down-the-line photographic sequence shows the "real" Hogan technique.

In my quest to help you develop a more consistent swing, I will explain the vital elements that made Hogan's swing work so well and I will reiterate some technical points. But mostly I will discuss the unique address, backswing, and downswing keys, based on my contact with Hogan and the observations of Hogan's swing I made while viewing a video of a Shell's Wonderful World of Golf match between Hogan and Sam Snead. I will include commentary from the game's most renowned teachers and tour players to better relay the instruction. I also will depend on the unique insights of others who have a good understanding of the swing and were close to Hogan in some way. Some of these individuals, such as Debbie Rivers, believe Hogan had more than one secret.

Rivers, an LPGA teaching professional and two-time Louisiana State Amateur champion, feels strongly that Hogan did not depend on just one swing secret, and she speaks authoritatively. She once received a lesson from Hogan inside the clubhouse grill-room of Shady Oaks, when she was visiting the famous club. Hogan gave her these tips as she listened intently, knowing she was one of the luckiest golfers in the world:

- Address the ball with the elbows close together;
- Set the right foot perpendicular to the target line;
- Keep the left arm stiff on the backswing and rotate the arms;
- On the downswing, rotate the left hip in a counter-clockwise direction as soon as possible (after making a lateral shift) and get the feeling of swinging from in to out.

Rivers asked Hogan one question: "Do you think about rotating your hips in a counterclockwise direction?" Hogan's answer: "I think about everything I do during the swing."

Another person, Mike McGetrick, one of *GOLF Magazine*'s top one hundred teachers in America, also believes Hogan had more than one secret.

"Hogan's secret was understanding the various elements of the setup and swing that allowed him to create an open clubface at impact and produce a highly controlled left-to-right fade," said McGetrick. "His keys include moving the left hand more to the left, fanning the clubface open in the takeaway to create a flatter swing plane, cupping his left wrist at the top of the swing, rotating and clearing his hips briskly early in the downswing, swinging into impact from a shallow angle of attack, and delaying the release of the golf club."

As you can gather by now, Hogan had more than one secret. To best appreciate what made Hogan's technique work so efficiently, it's critical that you analyze this master shotmaker's setup, since the nature of your starting position has a big bearing on the nature of your swing.

## The Address

From this unique down-target view, showing Hogan at address, one of the first things you will notice is how Hogan set the club down an inch behind the ball. Moe Norman, another of the most accurate shotmakers of all time, also sets up with a gap between the club and the ball. I recommend Hogan's setup to any player who swings the club back on a steep plane and chops down on the ball in the hitting area, because it promotes a low takeaway action. Even Hogan, who hinged his right wrist earlier than most players, did not pick up the club immediately at the start of the takeaway,

**A**nother of Hogan's "lost fundamentals" is setting up with the club an inch behind the ball. This position will encourage you to sweep the club back low to the ground at the very start of the swing.

knowing this fault hinders the turning and weight shifting actions of the body and causes a power loss in the swing.

Although Hogan's grip is very weak, he does not make the same mistake others often do when holding the club in this fashion—allowing his right arm to be above his left arm. He learned that this position causes you to swing the club back well outside the target line, then across it through impact. Therefore, set up with the right arm behind the left, and the right elbow pointing at the right hip. This position is very vital, because it encourages the right elbow to fold naturally at the top of the swing (rather than move too far away from the body or "fly"), with the funny bone virtually at a right angle to the ground. When the right elbow flies, there is a good chance the club will swing back on an exaggerated upright plane. This is what Jim McLean calls a "death move," because once you swing back this way you will have virtually no chance of swinging into the ball using a sweeping action, which is a vital key to hitting solid shots with the long clubs.

"Hogan's starting position set Hogan on the road to power," said Babe Bellagamba, a member of the United States Golf Teachers Federation who witnessed Hogan hit a drive over three-hundred yards at Cincinnati's Kenwood Country Club. "His right elbow position is a strong power source. Keeping the right elbow relatively close to the body in the takeaway forces the right wrist to hinge at the top of the swing, pulling the left wrist into a cupped position—bending backward and inward—

**61**

which opens the clubface. Keeping the elbows level with each other at the top, with the right one pointing more inward than outward, allowed Hogan to be poised to arrive in an excellent hitting position."

Another unique feature of Hogan's setup is that his shoulder position does not match that of his feet. This is another of Hogan's lost fundamentals, since he never mentioned it in any of his writings. Typically, teachers call for the shoulders and feet to be parallel to the target line, or "square," at address. They claim that when you start off square you have the best chance of being square at the top, and also delivering the center portion of the clubface to the back of the ball.

Hogan, being smart and inquisitive, discovered that the true sweet spot of the clubface was closer to the heel. He wanted this part of the club to contact the ball, since this kind of impact is more solid and helps impart a slight degree of cut-spin on the ball. Because he had this goal in mind, he set his feet in a closed position and his shoulders parallel to the target line. The closed-foot position helped him swing the club slightly to the inside, and then slightly outward toward the ball in the hitting area. Had his shoulder position matched his foot position, he would have blocked the ball out to the right. Had he set his shoulders open to the target line (aiming left), the tendency would have been to hook the ball or hit a pull slice. The square shoulder position, along with his firmer left-hand grip, helped him hold back the releasing action of the club and keep its face slightly open at impact.

When Hogan struggled with his game, he looked tense at address, setting his hands well away from his body and outstretching his arms. The new Hogan stood closer to the ball, keeping his hands several inches from his body. To further promote relaxation at address, Hogan bent his elbows slightly, the right more than the left, while allowing his arms to hang freely downward. By no means were the arms allowed to be limp like spaghetti, but they were relaxed. Hogan bent over slightly from the ball and socket joints of his hips, not from his waist, and flexed his knees a little. By keeping his legs straighter and bending more at the hips, Hogan created a sharper angle (about 30 degrees) between the legs and spine.

"This postural position ensures that you stand the right distance from the ball and enables the body to turn more freely going back and coming into the ball," says power-hitter Mike Dunaway. "It also creates the proper angle at address at which about 95 percent of all the work in the golf swing is done."

Rick Grayson, one of *GOLF Magazine*'s top one hundred teachers in America, agrees with Dunaway on the importance of good posture and the correct spine angle at address.

"Hogan was aware that how he set his spine would influence the plane of his swing," said Grayson. "If the spine is slightly erect, the shoulders will turn on the correct flatter plane. Hogan's elbows were also pointed inward. The left elbow pointed toward his left hip bone; the right elbow pointed toward the right hip bone. This positioning of the elbows to the hips linked Hogan's upper and lower body.

"When the spine is tilted forward, and the shoulders are humped over, the plane is too steep. If the spine is straight, you have not bent enough from the hips, which is another postural fault that leads to mishit shots. If the elbows point outward and are too far apart when a player takes his or her address, the tendency is to swing the club along an exaggerated outside-to-inside path and slice the ball. Hogan swung the club on inside-square-inside path, although even he admitted that he felt he swung on an inside-outside path, seemingly because he delayed the releasing action of the club until the last split second of the downswing."

Geoff Bryant, president of the United States Golf Teachers Federation, believes Hogan's technically correct address gave onlookers a hint of the tremendous sequel of mechanical swing perfection to come.

"Hogan was able to swing the club on-plane, almost as if he were a mechanical robot, because of the same good posture he established when addressing the ball," said Bryant.

The address apparently seems unimportant to most golfers, because when I watch average players set up they tend to pay more attention to being comfortably unorthodox rather than correct. The fact is, you can never consistently hit the ball powerfully and accurately unless you set up in a balanced fashion, with good posture and the clubface aimed squarely at the target.

Hogan, like all top-notch professionals, was very

meticulous about setting up. Jack Nicklaus is a prime example of a player who knows the value of a good address position. Nicklaus swings differently than Hogan, but when it comes to aiming the club he believes what Hogan believed: If you set up correctly, you stand a good chance of hitting a fairly good shot, even if your swing is a little off. If you address the ball incorrectly, you will probably hit an off-line shot, even if you make a technically sound swing.

When Hogan set up he gave the impression of purposefulness and power, owing to his perfect balance and the secure way he set his hands. He set his hands higher than in his early years, with the wrists arched slightly. This unique position was a safeguard against the left wrist breaking down at impact, the right hand taking control, the clubface becoming closed, and the shot hooking.

When Hogan swung the club he coordinated the movements of the body musically, as if conducting some kind of physiological symphony. We'll analyze those movements now, since there is no better model of technical perfection.

## The First Movement

Hogan uses his hands to waggle the club and make the transition into the takeaway, while bringing the clubface slightly inside the target line. It's important to note, though, that during his heyday Hogan calmed down his waggle, hinging only his right wrist dramatically, rather

In the First Movement Hogan makes a smooth transition from the waggle to the takeaway.

than both of them. Hogan believed waggling the club the same way each time relaxed him and triggered a flowing swing, just as actors like Christopher Walken and Jack Nicholson believe a familiar habitual physical gesture, such as touching an ear, helps the tempo of the words flow.

Watching Hogan aim the club at his target and waggle the club is like watching an expert marksman getting ready to shoot a gun. In waggling the club, Hogan was pre-rehearsing the right-wrist hinge that was to occur first late in the takeaway then more strikingly at the top of the swing. PGA Tour player Mark O'Meara, who models his swing after Hogan's, employs the very same waggle.

At this point in the swing, Hogan also keeps his right knee flexed and his head dead still to avoid swaying and throwing his body off balance. His straight right-foot position—toe-end perpendicular to the target line—puts a governor on his hip turn, preventing them from over-turning. Notice how still the right hip is at this point in the swing. Hogan wants to limit the turning action of the hip to avoid swinging on an overly flat plane and to create power by building resistance between the upper and lower body. Hogan is also very careful not to turn his shoulders on an exaggerated flat plane, for fear that the club will swing too far behind his body and so far inside the target line that it will be difficult to deliver the face into the ball correctly.

What you cannot see from the photograph is the tempo of Hogan's swing. It was not as deliberate as that of his fellow players, because Hogan believed that starting the club back too slowly, rather than smoothly, threw off the rhythm of the swing. Hogan's swing tempo was also slightly faster than that of his contemporaries because he used his hands more than they did. Still, he was in full control because he had such a great feel for the clubhead. This was not something he was born with. The early improvising Hogan did on the practice ground, using just a five-iron to hit a variety of shots, helped him develop this feel. Furthermore, he learned from great pianists that drinking ginger ale helps take the puffiness out of the fingers, thereby enhancing feel.

## The Second Movement

Hogan uses his hands and arms to swing the club farther inside the target line. Yet, the clubhead is in the ideal toe-up position, because of Hogan's very weak right-hand grip. In Hogan's early playing days, a strong finger grip caused him to exaggerate hand action and swing the club back incorrectly.

From this angle, you can clearly see how Hogan's right hand stays on top of the club. This weak hold prevents him from turning his hands over (a position in which the back of the left hand and the right palm would face the sky). This fault was a feature of the old Hogan swing and one that caused him to hit a severe duck-hook.

Hogan is still controlling this action with his hands, albeit more smoothly than quickly. We know this is true

In the Second Movement Hogan keeps his right hand on top of the club, knowing this is very critical to promoting a fade and preventing a hook.

because, even though the club has swung to the inside, the right hip is still dead square to the target and the shoulders have only turned slightly in a clockwise direction.

Hogan maintains the flex in his right knee, knowing that if he straightens it he will make a faulty hip turn and swing the club well above or below his normal plane-line.

If you look at Hogan's right wrist, you will see that it is only slightly hinged. Hogan pushes the club back with the left hand, rather than pulling it back with the right. This push-action encourages him to swing the club farther back, well past the right side of his body, and creates a wide, powerful swing arc.

## The Third Movement

This is the square position all golfers should strive for at this stage of the swing. The clubface, the palm of the right hand, and the back of the left hand all face the target line.

Hogan hinges his right wrist to enhance his feel for the clubhead, which remains in the classic toe-up position. Hogan's tucked right-elbow position helps him swing the club on-plane.

According to Robert Baker, a Master Teaching Professional at *GOLF Magazine*, "hinging the right wrist 90 degrees is a hidden power source that Hogan tapped into."

Johnny Miller, who like Hogan used a weak grip and constantly hit shots on target, also believed in the benefits of hinging the right wrist at this point in the swing. I

**70**

In the Third Movement Hogan hinges the right wrist; he discovered this action to be a hidden source of power in the
swing.

spoke with Miller about this action in the early 1980s when we both worked at *GOLF Magazine*. He thought hinging the wrist enhanced Hogan's feel for where the club was at certain points in the swing and made him swing at maximum efficiency. He also believed the right-wrist set was more natural and a vital conduit to generating power in the swing, particularly when employed in synchronization with the hinging of the right arm at the elbow. Miller told me that hinging the right wrist and arm, then unhinging them late in the downswing, adds snap to the swing, and maximizes power at impact. To back up this point, read what this fine shotmaker said in his book, *Pure Golf*.

Winding up the right arm and wrist is essential in just about all athletic actions and golf is no exception. There's no doubt that the right hand and arm have to hit and hit hard. I'm firmly convinced that there are more problems caused by an inactive right arm and wrist than practically anything else in the golf swing. The only provision is that the left side has to pull down first—then you can release the angles in the right arm and wrist as hard as you can.

## The Fourth Movement

Hogan stays balanced because he keeps his left foot on the ground and his head rock-steady. Good balance al-

In the Fourth Movement Hogan's right hip begins coiling in a clockwise direction, triggering a weight shift into his right foot and leg.

lows him to stay in control and swing the club on the proper inside path.

Hogan's left knee starts moving outward toward the ball as a result of his hips starting to turn and weight shifting from his left side to his right side.

Hogan continues to push the club back past his body to create the desired wide swing arc, another element of power.

## The Fifth Movement

If a laser were shot through the shaft of Hogan's club, starting at the clubhead end, it would channel through the shaft and burn a hole in the ground behind the ball, at a point precisely on the target line. This evidence proves that Hogan had, up until this point, swung the club perfectly on-plane. When you swing the club back, try to match Hogan's Fifth Movement position shown on page 75. If the imaginary laser hits a point outside the target line, it tells you that your swing is too flat. If the laser hits a point inside the target line, you know your swing is too upright.

Once again, we see that Hogan has stayed connected and kept the club nicely in the toe-up position. As has been the case so far, his head remains still and the left arm close to the body. The right elbow has stayed close to his body, too.

What I would like you to study here is the position of Hogan's left knee. It starts to make its move farther out-

PLANE LINE

TARGET LINE

**I**n the Fifth Movement Hogan swings the club perfectly on-plane. We know this to be true because the shaft line hits the target line.

ward toward the ball, as a result of Hogan's more active hip turn and weight-shift action.

## The Sixth Movement

If you were to look at one thousand photographs of Hogan's backswing during the time he played his best golf, they would all be virtually identical.

"Hogan put the club in the exact same backswing slot practically every time, because, without fail, he swung his left arm across his chest," said Julius Richardson of the United States Golf Teachers Federation.

Hogan grooved this position by practicing swinging to the three-quarter point while trying to keep a club-head cover tucked under his left armpit. High-handicap golfers tend to let the left arm move away from the chest. Consequently, they swing the club back well outside the plane line and slice across the ball in the hitting area. If you have this problem, the same drill that helped Hogan will help you.

Believe it or not, this is as far back as you will see Hogan swing with a medium or long iron. Moreover, unless he was trying to hit the ball extra hard, he employed virtually the same length swing with the driver or any other wood. Hogan was one of the original three-quarter swingers. Because he was so savvy, I wonder if, during the 1950s when his game was in top form, he knew what recent test surveys show: you can generate as much club-

In the Sixth Movement Hogan puts the club in the ideal back-swing position, swinging his left arm across his chest and pointing his right elbow downward.

head velocity with a compact swing as you can swinging back to the parallel position.

Hogan's shoulders have turned nicely on a slightly flatter plane than his arms, something every golfer should concentrate on doing, although Hogan never mentioned this in his writings. British-based teacher John Jacobs writes this in his book *Practical Golf*:

> It is a common misconception, even among good golfers, that the shoulders and arms should move on the same plane in the backswing. If the arms are to position the club correctly in the back-swing, and swing freely in the through-swing, they must swing up as the shoulders turn around. Trying to marry your arms to your shoulders introduces too much body action into the shot, at the expense of clubhead speed.

Hogan's shoulders have turned more than his hips, an action that is a definite source of power. Hogan's left shoulder has turned fully under his chin, another movement you should emulate since it is a secret to coiling the upper body and generating power.

Hogan is in full control of the club, too, thanks to his improved grip. Here, you can see that his right forefinger fits snugly between the first two fingers of his left hand. The finger is not draped loosely across his first and second fingers, as was the case when he was suffering from off-line duck-hook shots.

If you look closely at Hogan's left arm, wrist, and hand, you can see that there is a small indentation between the left forearm and the back of the left hand. This is very subtle, but if you were to take a pencil and draw a line along the top of the forearm, then continue tracing this path, you would see that the line moves upward as it hits the back of the hand, making the concave "cup" in the wrist visible.

Many teachers advocate a flat position of the left wrist because it indicates that the clubface is also square in relation to the arc of the swing. The cupped position at the top means the clubface is slightly open. Like Hogan, Tiger Woods and Fred Couples cup their left wrist, for fear of duck-hooking. In fact, Couples told me this: "I prefer the cupped position, which indicates a slightly open clubface, because I know that on the downswing I can really let my wrists whip into the ball with no fear of hitting a wild hook. I think, therefore, that the cupped position ultimately results in a more powerful golf shot."

Hogan's right wrist is hinged virtually to the maximum, because through practice he learned that this position sets a player up for the latest possible hit. David Duval is another example of a golfer who hinges the right wrist, believing this swing action promotes added power into his swing. What Duval and other pros realize is that your wrist position at the top has a big influence on where in the swing you release power and transmit energy into the clubhead via the arms and hands. In days past, Bobby Jones increased his wrist hinge at the top of the swing in order to set himself up for a late club-to-ball snap.

## The Seventh Movement

The reason Hogan makes such a quick transition into the downswing is because he created so much torque between the upper and lower body on the backswing. Also, the second he reaches the top of the swing, he shifts his hips laterally toward the target.

In Hogan's estimation this lower-body action was one of his swing secrets. I know this because Hogan spoke at length about this movement at the New York Waldorf-Astoria in 1988, and, at the end of the Shell's Wonderful World of Golf videotape mentioned earlier, commentator Gene Sarazen asked Hogan, "What's the most important thing in the swing?"

"You must let the lower body lead the downswing—the hips and knees—then release the club near the bottom," said Hogan. "Most amateurs rotate the shoulders first, causing them to hit across the ball and hit the outside of it instead of the back of it."

From the following remarks, you can see that teacher Jim McLean also believes that good lower-body action was critical to Hogan's success:

> In 1969–1971, during the time I was studying and playing golf for the University of Houston team, friends of mine called me to tell me when Hogan was going to play Shady Oaks. This was a shotmaking exhibition and learning experience I did not want to miss, since at the time I already had aspirations of playing tour golf or teaching. So

**80**

In the Seventh Movement Hogan shifts and rotates his hips, allowing his hands and the club to drop down into the ideal hitting slot.

I packed my things and drove over to Fort Worth, Texas, to stay with my friend Jack Burke.

Watching Hogan hit shots was educational. Six or seven times I and only a few others who received a tip on the hottest ticket in town, stared in awe as Hogan played one masterful shot after another.

It is hard to single out one solitary secret. However, I am sure that one of the strongest elements of Hogan's swing was the way he moved his hips. At the start of the downswing, the hips moved laterally several inches, before they started rotating left so fast I only noticed a flash. This brisk clearing action of the hips helped Hogan whip the club into impact at high speed and hit the ball an average distance of 280 yards and, in the right conditions, 300 yards.

"I agree with McLean," said Greg Hood, a former personal assistant of Hogan's who often watched him practice at Shady Oaks.

According to Hood, Hogan was once asked by professional Bobby Clampett, a hot tour player in the early 1980s, how to lead the downswing with the right elbow pointing downward and inward and the right shoulder dropping to a good hitting position. Hogan's answer: "The lateral shift of the hips takes care of those things automatically. You don't put yourself in those positions."

In watching tapes of Hogan, Mike Mallon of the United States Golf Teachers Federation was also impressed by Hogan's lower-body action: "I was particularly struck by the way Hogan gently slid his hips laterally. He allowed his lower body to take command of the downswing while the upper body resisted. Right there is the reason he hit the ball solidly."

Shifting the hips laterally triggers the transfer of weight from Hogan's right side to his left side and gives the upper body a chance to catch up. The lateral move of the hips is difficult to spot when watching the pros play, yet it is common to all good golfers from the past and present.

I love the photograph of Hogan's start-down position because it clearly shows that his hips have practically returned to the exact position they were in at address—parallel to the target line. The reason you do not see the left hip is because it has not yet cleared. Even though Hogan called for an early clearance, he did not rotate the hips to the left of target until he had first shifted them laterally.

The other reason I admire this photograph is because it shows how Hogan drops the club on the desired shallower downswing plane—in what three-time Masters champion Jimmy Demaret called the "ready position." Demaret believed this move was Hogan's secret because it set him up for an on-plane delayed hit. This drop-down movement, the result of the lateral hip-shifting action, enables Hogan to change his pivot point from his right leg to his left leg, and to be poised to powerfully unwind the shoulders, the arms, the hands, and the club—in that order. The fact that his right foot comes off the ground for the first time in the swing, albeit only slightly, proves he has started to move into his left side.

"In 1950, I played with Hogan at the Bel-Air Country Club," said swing guru Mike Austin who is in the *Guinness Book of World Records* for hitting the longest drive of all time. "This was Hogan's first complete round of golf since recovering from the accident. Before the round, Hogan told me about a dream he had during his stay in the hospital. In the dream, Hogan saw himself pivoting around his left foot and leg, just like Jay Broune, an old Scottish pro. In the dream, Hogan hit one superbly controlled power-fade shot after another. Hogan told me he was going to try playing that way during his round with me. To shorten a long story, Hogan kept his word and proved to me that dreams can come true. He had the most efficient swing I had ever seen, and never once hit a bad hook shot. He was in full control of his game."

At this point in the swing, Hogan begins what top instructors call a body release. Hogan anchors himself around his left-leg pivot point, so he's readied to release his right hip and knee, and swing the club into the ball with the large muscles of the body controlling the action. When a player employs a full-body release, powerful leverage is retained in the swing because the legs resist rather than lurch toward the target. When the latter occurs, the tendency is to hit a big block.

## The Eighth Movement

This is a great delivery position. Hogan's right foot has begun to lift even more now, indicating that he has started to rotate his hips to the left of target and shifted weight to his left foot and leg. Notice that the left hip is visible for the first time, showing Hogan has begun to clear it.

"Therein lies the main applicator of this golfer's phenomenal distance-producing leverage, the cause of his prodigious extension of the arms and club toward the target, and the supplier of the momentum that sends the driver flying way up and around and down his back at the finish of the swing," writes Ken Bowden in *The Masters of Golf*.

Hogan's shoulders are slightly closed. He never lets the left shoulder clear too early or the right shoulder jut out, for fear of coming over the top and mishitting the ball. To keep his left shoulder in check, Hogan keeps his upper left arm snug to his body. To keep his right shoulder in check, he keeps his right elbow close to his body.

At this moment in the action, Hogan's right knee and right hip rotate toward the target. These body-release keys help Hogan generate high clubhead speed. "Every golfer should try to drive through with the right leg, just as Ben does," said Jimmy Demaret when analyzing Hogan's swing in 1978 for *GOLF Magazine*. Hogan's powerful right-sided action begins as he drops the club into the shallower hitting slot. The back of the left hand, the palm of the right, and the clubface all face the target line, indicating that Hogan's swing is perfectly on-plane.

It is absolutely incredible how long Hogan resists. While his left hip clears and his right knee moves inward, his right wrist maintains its strong hinged position. The club is still a long way from the ball.

In Hogan's Eighth Movement he actively clears his left hip to make room for his arms to deliver the club into the ball. He also squeezes his upper left arm against his body while holding the angle in his right wrist—two keys to accuracy and power.

"Hogan kept the club away from the ball as long as possible on the downswing, which has always been my philosophy," says golf instructor Phil Ritson. "Of course, eventually the club has to hit the ball. But, as Hogan proves, thinking of keeping the clubhead away from the ball makes you keep your hands, arms, and right shoulder back, rather than bringing them closer to the ball with that swing-wrecking over-the-top move called the early hit. Hogan's hit is very late, evidenced by how long his right wrist stays cocked on the downswing. He waits to the last moment to uncock his right wrist and to release the club into the ball. Consequently, stored power being released through the unwinding of the hips, shoulders, and body is mostly responsible for Hogan's extra-solid shots."

"This is a superb position," says Florida-based teacher Peter Croker. "Hogan is poised to push the club into and through the ball, using the right hand, right wrist, and right arm as sources of power and control."

Hogan makes sure his right hand stays behind the left. The last thing he wants the right hand to do is rotate over his left. Many novice golfers think they should do that to release the club. Don't, otherwise you will close the clubface at impact and hit a bad hook shot.

Hogan prevents the right hand from taking over by squeezing his upper left arm against his body and increasing the angle between the back of his left hand and his left wrist bone. Mike Adams, one of the game's most highly respected golf instructors, has firsthand knowledge that this was indeed Hogan's one and only secret to consistently keeping the clubface slightly open at impact and hitting a power-fade.

"In 1984, after watching Hogan hit about one hundred balls at Shady Oaks, I commented that the dish angle of his left wrist increased, becoming more concave as a result of keeping the upper part of his left arm tight to his chest on the downswing," said Adams.

According to Adams, Hogan paused, bent over to pick up his cigarette, then, before taking a drag, looked him right in the eyes and said, "Son, that's the secret."

## The Ninth Movement

I have included a drawing for you to look at, showing Hogan at the precise moment of impact. From this frontal angle, note the bow in Hogan's left wrist.

"The back of Hogan's left wrist is closer to the target than any other part of his hand," says Gerald McCullagh, one of *GOLF Magazine*'s top one hundred teachers in America. "There's no doubt that this one solitary move was Hogan's secret to keeping the clubface open slightly at impact and consistently hitting a power-fade shot."

I once asked legendary instructor Bob Toski about Hogan's secret and he agreed with McCullagh; Hogan's left-hand position better allowed him to hold the clubface open at impact and hit a controlled power-fade shot.

Although this move was easier for Hogan because he

In the Ninth Movement Hogan hits the ball powerfully, letting the left hand guide the club into impact and the right hand provide the power.

was a natural left-hander with added strength in that hand, average golfers will benefit by learning this power-action through hard practice. And, if a hook shot is your problem, you should try to match Hogan's right-elbow position. By bringing the right elbow down like Hogan, it is virtually impossible to close the clubface at impact.

At impact, the back of Hogan's left wrist faces the target, but the wrist bone is raised considerably because he is squeezing the grip with the last three fingers of his left hand. This added pressure allows the left hand to do all the guiding and the right hand to produce the hitting power.

## The Tenth Movement

By looking at Hogan in the through-impact position, you can see the awesome power and authority he had over his body and the club. Note, particularly, that both hips have cleared. This clearing action is necessary to open a path for the club to enter the impact zone. Hogan promotes this full-body release by allowing his head to start rotating slightly toward the target. More and more professionals and low-handicap amateur players are employing this type of head movement, knowing it helps a player clear his or her left hip more quickly and generate higher arm-hand-club speed.

There's another element to Hogan's swing that you should make a mental note of. Even after the strike, Hogan's club is low to the ground, proving that it ex-

In the Tenth Movement, the through-impact position, Hogan extends the club through the ball, letting his head rotate toward the target and his upper and lower body release fluidly.

tended along the target line before moving to the inside. Hogan's good arm extension is a critical connection to his creating a flat spot or extended area at the bottom of the swing, starting just before impact and ending just after impact. The longer the flat spot, the longer the clubface stays on the ball and the more power is produced.

Just look at the force created by Hogan's release—the unhinging of the right wrist and the straightening of the right arm. If you play right-handed, you can only arrive in this position if you allow the left hand to lead, the right to follow. The left hand guides the club into the ball, the right hand follows. The force generated by Hogan's body release is transferred to the hands, arms, and club. The end result is a super-powerful hit.

In viewing Hogan's powerful through-impact position, I agree with the following comment made by ABC television golf commentator Peter Alliss, in his book *Who's Who in Golf*:

> No one before or since has matched the low drive through the hitting area with his right hand that was the hallmark of the Hogan swing. He had reached perhaps the nearest any golfer has come to mastery over the ball.

Legendary player Sam Snead also voiced his praise for Hogan's right-side action in an interview with Peter Kessler on The Golf Channel. "Hogan's right-arm extension straight through the ball is what allowed him to make solid contact," said Snead.

Ken Butler, of the United States Golf Teachers Federation agrees: "Keeping his right arm extended through impact allowed Hogan to keep the club on the ball a moment longer, which is one definite secret to hitting powerful shots."

## The Eleventh Movement

In looking at the photograph of Hogan's follow-through on page 94, notice the light dirt thrown in the air. There has been no thick chunk of turf taken out of the ground. Hogan was known to practically pick the ball cleanly off the grass. He accomplished this by swinging down on a much shallower arc. Hogan preferred to swing this way, knowing if he were to go down after the ball aggressively, grass and dirt would probably fill the grooves of the clubface, causing the shot to fly uncontrollably another 10 to 20 yards, with no backspin.

Pay attention, too, to how Hogan's head has rotated further toward the target, with his eyes looking down the line. Again, Hogan's head rotation helps him make a full-body release and put a lot of oomph behind the shot. Every amateur player would do well to note how complete Hogan's follow-through is. As former British Open champion Henry Cotton said in the book *A History of Golf Illustrated*, "Few golfers hit past the chin and under the head better than Hogan."

When I study Hogan's powerful follow-through, I vividly recall the following statement Al Laney of the *Paris Herald* made in his book *Following the Leaders*: "It is

In the Eleventh Movement Hogan follows through brilliantly, with his right shoulder rotating past his chin.

easy to forget Hogan was one of the longest hitters when he wanted to be." Obviously, Laney said this because he knew golfers around the world associated Hogan more with accuracy than with power.

## The Twelfth Movement

Finish positions do not get better than this. Hogan is the perfect example of relaxed balance. The next time you check yourself on video, make sure you match these positions of Hogan's:

- Hands high above the head, with both of them married comfortably together as a unit, just as they were at address
- Both arms folded, the left more than the right, with the left elbow pointing directly at the ground
- All but the toe-end of the right foot off the ground
- Body facing a point just left of target
- Eyes looking directly down the target line
- Left leg straight
- Right knee flexed
- Body erect
- The majority of your weight on the heel and outer portion of the left foot

**I**n the Twelfth Movement Hogan's superb balance proves that he has swung the club with maximum efficiency.

# 4

## Practice with a Purpose

•

Creative practice taught
Hogan—and will teach you—how to
become an inventive shotmaker

---

The following story, still kicked around in country club grillrooms, will tell you all you need to know about Hogan the perfectionist and his attitude toward practice.

One year at the Rochester Open, Hogan shot 64, with a double bogie on his card. After the round, Hogan went to the practice tee, while fellow tour pros Jimmy Demaret, Craig Wood, and Lloyd Mangrum retired to the nineteenth hole for drinks and a game of high-stakes gin.

Hours later, when it was almost dark, the aforesaid trio left the bar and noticed someone practicing. Curious, they approached. The man hitting balls was Hogan. Demaret asked: "Ben, you just hit a 64 with ten birdies on your scorecard, what are you doing here?"

Hogan's reply: "Jimmy, there's no reason why a man can't birdie every hole."

During his early amateur and professional days, Hogan was not such a big fan of practice. But eventually he grew to love practice and the challenge of discovering a new swing key that would turn his hook into a fade. Moreover, in time, he learned to face up to one golfing fact: once you develop a good swing technique, it only stays with you if you practice regularly and purposefully.

"Practice was Hogan's secret formula to success, because he wanted to hit the ideal shot, not just a good shot," said Bill Picca, a master professional for the United States Golf Teachers Federation.

Hogan reached the point where he spent all his waking hours off the course practicing golf, believing that the player himself, and no one else, has to be able to fix a fault. Even when not hitting balls, I'm told he often sat alone in a kind of trance, gesturing with his hands, as if going over a secret movement in his mind.

On the practice tee, Hogan concentrated intently on every shot he played, as if he were competing in a major championship and that particular shot meant the difference between winning and losing. No wonder his fellow pros and amateur fans used to gather around him. They thought they could learn more by watching this master craftsman at work than by hitting ball after ball in search of an answer to the mystery of the swing. In their minds, based on Hogan's track record, he had already discovered "it."

No matter how well you once played the game, or how good you are now, you will never keep your game tuned and in form if you fail to practice hard and with a purpose. What's meant by this is practicing with an on-course mindset and sticking to a preswing routine. Even in practice, Hogan maintained the same deep level of concentration, looking hard at the target and carefully examining the flight of the ball. Moreover, the man the Scots nicknamed the Wee Iceman for his steely nerves, followed the same routine before he hit a shot. He took one practice swing to the side of the ball. Next, holding the club in his right hand only, he stepped into the shot, right foot first, while staring at the target. Next, he placed the club down, behind the ball slightly, dead square to it and the target. Next, he placed his left foot down next to his right. Next, he gripped the club with his left hand. Next, he spread his feet apart and squeezed the club with the pressure fingers of his left hand three times. Next, he waggled the club three times, while casting his eyes from target to ball the same number of times. When staring at the target, he visualized a tunnel that curved to the right slightly, along the same line as the intended flight of the ball. Finally, he started the club back smoothly with his hands.

Practicing with a purpose also means working on weaknesses in your shotmaking game, not just on your strengths, and aiming at a target. According to Jim McLean, Ben Hogan and all good players stare at the target and glance at the ball, while poor players stare at the ball and glance at the target.

Depending on when Hogan practiced—before a round, after a round, or when he was away from the course—he followed a very different routine, yet his sessions were always businesslike. When Hogan practiced, he always had a serious singular goal in mind. If he was confused about something technically, he knew he would have to solve a swing problem by "digging it out of the dirt," even it meant hitting balls until his hands bled. Hogan possessed a passion for practice because he was constantly looking for new ways to improve. You amateurs will gain greatly by adopting the same attitude.

"There was a quality to Hogan's practice beyond anything I had ever seen," said Michael Murphy the author of the spiritual book, *Golf in the Kingdom*, during a *Golf Digest* interview with renowned golf writer Lorne Rubenstein.

"Hogan used to play the Crosby and in the evening practice at Pebble Beach. It was exhilarating. Hogan would begin to practice and slowly people would gather to watch. One day I noticed more and more pros, at least 20 of them, maybe 200 people more, sitting together in a semicircle. There was absolute silence. The sun was going down and darkness was falling and Hogan was hitting six-irons to a caddie. The caddie was not moving. Hogan would raise his hand now and then, meaning that the ball was going to bean the caddie. The caddie would look up slightly and step aside.

"Darkness fell and the silence deepened as Hogan hit balls. We all walked away when it was over. Nobody spoke. I will never forget it. It imprinted me. The depth of his practice imprinted me, the joy of it. I was maybe 15 or 16—it made an impression that I will never forget. It was the love, the enchantment, of practice.

"Hogan's practice sessions worked their magic on me,

all right, and in a deeply felt way. They helped me see that golfers, and others as well, are capable of transformative discipline. Such practice can make something beautiful happen."

Let's now look at how Hogan practiced creatively and developed into such a fine swinger and shotmaker.

## Hogan's Preround Practice Routine

Most pros begin their practice sessions by stretching their muscles, either by swinging two or three clubs at once, or by holding the club behind the back with arms extended, then rotating the body back and forth from the hips, Jack Nicklaus style. Next, they hit a few sand-wedge shots off grass. Next, they hit even-numbered irons, starting with the pitching wedge (10-iron), or odd-numbered irons starting with the sand iron (11-iron). Next, they hit some 3-wood shots and drives, before moving onto the putting green. Surprisingly, the majority of pros do not practice chips or sand shots before a round, unless the tournament is being contested on a course with very heavy fringe, such as a U.S. Open venue, or very different type of sand, such as a British Open links.

Surprisingly, too, some tour pros don't go through a planned regular routine. They simply "rake" a ball over to a spot near them, set up quite quickly, then swing. Hogan, by contrast, was much more methodical in his approach to practice.

During his winning days on tour, Hogan was a very

flexible individual, so he didn't need to do any preround exercises to get loose. He would, however, begin his sessions by hitting full 9-iron shots, using his normal swing. This club is much shorter and more lofted than the long irons and woods, and requires less clubhead speed to hit crisply, so it is ideal for oiling the golf muscles.

When Hogan practiced, he separated himself from the rest of the players, either going to a solitary spot at an end of the practice tee or finding a shady area under a tree. Hogan was not interested in hearing about the nighttime ventures of his fellow players, watching them hit trick shots, or sharing jokes with them. He was interested in sharpening his game for the task at hand: winning the tournament he was competing in.

After hitting a few 9-iron shots, Hogan visualized specific holes on the course and mentally reviewed the key shots he would need to execute while playing them. He would then start practicing those tee-to-green shots. Wherever Hogan competed, he went through an entirely different pregame practice routine than his fellow players. They merely warmed up. He simulated the on-course experience to such a degree that he felt superconfident and superprepared by the time he arrived on the first tee to begin a competitive round of eighteen holes.

Hogan was a great preround planner, with a vivid imagination. When he played in the Masters, at the Augusta National Golf Club course, he knew that by hitting a right-to-left flying tee shot on the second hole, the ball would hit a big slope in the fairway. Hitting this slope would allow him to pick up enough added yardage to go

Hogan usually practiced away from other players, concentrating as intently as he would when competing in a tournament. He paid particular attention to the flight of the ball since that would warn him of any faults in his swing.

for the par-5 in two shots and set up an eagle putt. So, before a round at Augusta, he practiced this shot over and over until he was confident he could play it. Technically, this was tough, because Hogan was used to hitting the fade, not a draw. All the same, by neutralizing his grip, taking the cup out of his left wrist at the top of the swing, starting down by clearing his hips, and speeding his hand-arm-club release, he was able to hit controlled draw shots.

While on Augusta's practice tee, Hogan also spent more time practicing hitting high-medium and long irons, since these shots are needed on par-3's and on approach shots to par-4 holes to hold the firm greens. To play these shots Hogan simply positioned the ball more forward in his stance, opposite the left heel.

Other shots Hogan devoted time to, because they are so common at the National, were the short cut-spin pitch, played by swinging on an out-to-in path; and the running pitch, played by swinging on an exaggerated inside-to-inside path.

The greens are lightning fast at Augusta, too, so whenever Hogan played there he would allow time to practice hitting lag putts, usually just swinging more slowly than normal for the distance at hand. Since speed is more important to have a handle on than judging break, Hogan would practice hitting putts across the green, paying close attention to just how fast the ball rolled. He would make a mental note of the speed of the ball so that when he played the course competitively, he knew exactly how much softer to hit the ball in order to lag it close to the hole.

**H**ogan was fanatical about preparing properly for a tournament round. For example, before a round at Augusta National during Masters week, he would hit putts across the green, aiming at nothing. Since Augusta's greens have always been notoriously fast, and speed affects break, Hogan figured it was best to hit putts and watch the ball roll across the putting surface.

Of course, Hogan played at different courses around the United States, each requiring different shots. So, in preparing for a round, he practiced accordingly. When he was competing on courses where the wind is known to blow harder, such as in Chicago and Texas, he practiced diligently to perfect a shot that would help him beat the strong breezes. If Hogan played in Florida, he would spend extra time practicing trouble shots out of Bermuda grass and putting on greens with this type of rough-textured surface. When in the Carolinas, he was known to hit shots off pine needles, in an area of trees by the manicured practice area, just in case he should miss the fairway and find the ball perched atop pine needles. When practicing before a round in the U.S. Open, he spent a good amount of time "blasting" shots out of heavy fringe grass, as he would in sand, since it was inevitable he would probably face this shot at least once during a round. And the one time he played in the British Open, the 1953 championship at Scotland's Carnoustie Golf Club, he devoted most of his practice time to hitting sand shots since the texture of the sand was so different and the lips of the bunkers so high. To handle this situation, Hogan laid the clubface wide open, played the ball more forward in his stance than normal, picked the club up more quickly on the backswing, and hit down more aggressively.

Hogan just didn't step up and hit shots, either. Whatever club he selected, and whatever shot he practiced, he methodically settled into the setup. Before he hit the ball, Hogan carefully jockeyed himself into position, making sure his weight was distributed correctly, his hands were positioned properly on the club, his stance was right for the type of shot he was about to play, and his clubface and body alignment were also spot-on.

Each time, before he swung the club back, Hogan stared at a specific target, just like he planned to do on the course. Usually, a shag bag held by his caddy was the target. Hogan would tell the caddy to move left or right, backwards or forwards. After pinpointing the target with his eyes, Hogan waggled the club back and forth, in typical fashion, before starting the swing. Again, the waggle was his link to making a smooth transition from the setup to the takeaway, in practice and in play. Time after time, Hogan's shots landed at the caddy's feet.

Once Hogan's practice was over, he would walk to the first tee in a cocoon of concentration, not saying a word to anyone.

Hogan, as you can see, did not miss a trick. He was the most prepared of any of his fellow competitors, which is why at the end of the day he usually returned the lowest score.

## Hogan's Postround Practice Routine

If you have ever attended a golf tournament, you know that almost all pros return to the practice area after the round is over and they've turned in their scorecard. Until Hogan came along, players went straight to the locker room, the restaurant, the bar, or their car. They never hit shots after the round was over. Hogan was the first to do

**W**hen preparing for a round on a windy course, say in Texas, Hogan practiced hitting low shots.

this. When he started this postround practice routine, the pros laughed at him. That stopped when Hogan started to dominate, and all but a few followed his example.

Most rounds of Hogan's were good rounds. Still, he was such a perfectionist that the main purpose of Hogan's postround practice sessions revolved around damage control. Before he began to practice, Hogan could be seen sitting in a chair smoking a cigarette, all the time, one assumed, reviewing the round to figure out what, if anything, went a tiny bit wrong, and how he could correct a fault in the swing or figure out something that would allow him to hit shots even better than he had done on the course. Hogan was so disciplined that, no matter how well or poorly he played, he returned to the practice tee, anxious to improve his swing and shot-making game. Hogan hated quick fixes and depending on a teacher. He believed in figuring swing problems out for himself.

Hogan was never short of creativity. For example, if he determined that his swing had been too long on the course, and his tempo too fast, he would return to a quiet corner of the practice area and attempt to hit drives the same distance he normally hit 5-iron shots. Practicing this drill is a good way to promote a compact swing and correct an overly fast tempo that can cause you to mishit the ball, usually to the left of target.

Hogan's postround practice sessions were quite short, though he was known to hit balls until sundown if he was not really satisfied with an aspect of his game. Most often, at least in his later years, putting was the part of the game he worked on most. If, for example, missed short putts were costing him strokes on the course, he would practice them over and over, from all sides of the hole, until he was confident he had ironed out a fault or a bad mental attitude, readying himself for the next day's play.

Hogan was always looking for ways to improve and be one up on his fellow competitors. And he thought of everything, as this story will bear out.

After a tiring round in the heat of summer, Hogan drank a mild refreshment, then practiced hard on the range. After about an hour, a voice in the gallery of golf enthusiasts asked perplexingly, "Ben, aren't you tired? Why don't you give it a rest?" Hogan said, "I want to know how I swing and hit the ball when I'm tired."

## Hogan's Off-the-Course Practice Routine

Hitting shots on a strip of land between two fairways at Shady Oaks or practicing at Seminole Golf Club were enjoyable pastimes for Hogan when he was away from the tour because they offered him special challenges. The strip of land was very narrow so he had to concentrate hard and swing correctly to keep his shots on this "fairway." Hogan practiced at the Oaks in the late afternoon, which he enjoyed because it offered him some privacy. Solitary practice gave him time to keep his swing grooved or to try new shots that might help him shoot lower scores. Hogan liked Seminole because it was long enough and tough enough to present a challenge. Plus,

The main purpose of Hogan's postround practice was "damage control." Most of the time he played exceptionally well. But on days when he did not, he spent time tracing a fault in his technique and finding a solution. For example, if short putts gave him problems during a round, he would retire to the putting green and hit putts until he had regained confidence in his stroke.

it featured many of the windy conditions he was likely to encounter during tournament play.

Hogan also liked to stand beneath one of the shady trees and practice. Just as he did before a round of golf, he began these sessions by hitting 9-iron shots. The only difference was that he'd usually go through his entire bag of clubs and not switch from one club to the next until he was satisfied he had mastered the one in his hand. The driver was the last club he would hit.

On iron shots, he would look at the distance the ball traveled with each club and the shape of the shot, to monitor the plane and path of his swing. By looking at the depth of the divots left by the club slicing through the turf, Hogan could track the tempo of his swing. Hogan was most concerned with swinging too fast; if the divots he left were deep, he'd know that's what he had been doing.

The shot that Hogan would normally practice most was the power-fade, since that was the shot he depended on most, both off the tee and from the fairway. Often, to get in the mood to play this shot, and to set up a challenge, Hogan practiced fading the ball around trees. He also always practiced in a right-to-left wind, because this encouraged him to work the ball into it, using the fade. Hogan never practiced in a left-to-right wind. Through experience, he deduced that this wind condition magnified his fade, and caused him to start opening his body alignment too much, to adjust, or start playing hooks to fight the wind. Hogan also never practiced hitting shots downwind, because the lack of air resistance took the

When practicing, Hogan often hit fades around trees to stimulate his shotmaking imagination.

spin off the ball, thus disguising bad shots. Hogan did not like that. He wanted to honestly assess the quality of his shotmaking game.

When practicing at home, Hogan enjoyed hitting sand shots and trying out new methods. Occasionally, when a major was around the corner and it was very quiet at Shady Oaks, he would empty a shag bag of balls into a bunker and practice hitting long bunker shots. Hogan paid particular attention to this shot, since it is one of the toughest in golf, and one he was bound to face in a U.S. Open or PGA championship. In one session, he might change from a weak grip to a strong grip, or from a long upright swing to a short flat swing. He also experimented with different types of sand wedges, paying close attention to the depth of the bounce. Bounce means the degree to which the back or rear edge of the flange lies below the leading edge of the flange when the clubshaft is held in a perfectly vertical position. The bounce feature is unique to a sand wedge. The purpose of bounce is to allow the flange to glide through the sand like a knife through butter. If a sand wedge did not feature bounce, the leading edge would dig into the sand behind the ball, muffling the shot and perhaps leaving the ball in the bunker.

In practice, Hogan hit shots with different degrees of bounce, to see which performed best off tight fairway grass, out of rough, out of fringe grass, and in what type of sand. Typically, for shots out of average fluffy sand with a fairly firm base, Hogan selected a sand wedge with standard bounce, in the range of 10 to 14 degrees. In hard, crusty sand, Hogan chose a sand wedge with less than 10 degrees of bounce, or even a pitching wedge. For shots out of soft sand, he selected a sand wedge with more than 14 degrees of bounce.

Hogan worked on his putting, too, although early in his career he was the best putter on tour. He spent time trying out new putters and figuring out how much wrist action he needed to incorporate into his stroke. On longer putts Hogan depended on wrist action for feel and to get the ball rolling better on the slow greens of his day. Later in his career, when green speeds quickened, he used an all-arms putting stroke. Hogan once tried a split-grip putting hold that worked well. But he was such a traditionalist and fundamentalist that he stubbornly refused to use this grip on the course when playing in front of a tournament gallery. My advice is to learn from Hogan's mistake. If something unorthodox works, and you can repeat it consistently, stay with it.

Depending on the state of his game, Hogan would spend more or less time practicing. Usually, though, according to Greg Hood, his practice sessions lasted around two hours, with the main focus being to keep his power-fade shot grooved. In playing this shot, Hogan hit shots out of all kinds of lies, everything from a divot hole to deep rough, so that he was prepared for anything come competition time. Hogan also liked to finish off his practice sessions by playing a couple of holes, hitting two or three balls on each but rarely putting out.

To show you how good Hogan was and how much practice pays off, let me share with you a story told to me by Hood that has nothing to do with the formal record book.

In 1981, a film crew visited Shady Oaks to shoot a television commercial for Ben Hogan Apex II golf clubs with Hogan. The director told Hood that the shooting might take a couple of hours because they wanted to get the perfect "take"—showing the ball landing past the hole and spinning back about 20 feet, next to the cup. Hood relayed this message to his boss.

"Greg, just come for me when they're ready to shoot. . . . I'm not going to need a lot of time," said Hogan.

Hood told the director what Hogan said and he instantly became very nervous, knowing the difficulty of the 9-iron shot Hogan was expected to hit.

When the time came, Hood drove Hogan out to hole number one. Hogan quietly stepped out of the cart with a 9-iron in his hand, walked over to the spot the crew asked him to hit the shot from, set up, swung, and hit the perfect shot—the first time! "Let's go," was all Hogan said to Hood before the two of them took off in the cart. The director and crew stood behind frozen in shock.

This was not the only time Hogan shocked camera crews. During the filming of *Follow the Sun*, the movie about his accident and life on the tour, Hogan stood in for actor Glen Ford on certain full swings. There were no retakes then, either. Face it, Hogan was a true golfing machine.

# 5

## One Step Beyond

•

Studying Hogan's on-course habits
will help you develop good
course-management skills, enhance
your mental game, and allow you to
become a more consistent player

When conversations about Hogan switch from his masterful technique to the subject of course management, one discovers the importance of the mental game and the role it plays in the evolution of a player. Maybe you can't make the ball move with your mind, but you can think your way to lower scores. Hogan never approached the game with a negative mindset. He planned out each and every shot. I believe players can shave several strokes off their score by using their heads on the golf course, just like Hogan did.

Few golf aficionados know that Hogan was one of the top oilmen in Texas. I've heard he studied geological maps intently and got a kick out of beating the other big boys by finding a superstrike. In competition he was the same way. Hogan looked constantly for ways to beat the course. He loved to bring tough tracks "down to their knees."

Hogan's strategic preparation started before the round. He drove to the course extra slowly to help relax his mind and body. On arriving at the course where a tour event was being held, Hogan went into the locker room and sat quietly meditating. When he did move, he moved at a snail's pace. He even took extra time to tie his shoes because he discovered this strategy helped him to further relax. I'm told Hogan had a light breakfast, but would refrain from drinking coffee before a championship round, for fear of throwing off his metabolism and exciting his nervous system. Caffeine can be very dangerous to your game. It tends to make one excitable, so it can speed up your swing tempo and interfere with the strategic thought process.

Before a competitive round, Hogan also made sure he had plenty of new balls and tees. Ball markers, Band-Aids, a couple of clean towels, and an umbrella were other items on Hogan's checklist. All this preparation was part of Hogan's strategy. He felt that by being super-organized he could be one or two strokes up on the field of players before the championship ever began.

Hogan was very inventive. In the 1950 U.S. Open, for example, he took his favorite 7-iron out of the bag to make room for a 1-iron, knowing that "the knife" would come in more handy, and that if he carried both clubs he would go over the 14-club limit. If Hogan faced a 7-iron shot on the course, he figured he could simply take a 6-iron and make a shorter, slower swing.

Before walking to the first tee, Hogan made sure the caddy polished his clubs. Hogan paid particular attention to the grooves on his irons, since they need to be clean in order to impart spin on the ball. Hogan knew that one unforced error could cause him to mess up one hole and lose the tournament. Hogan thus adopted the sensible "better safe than sorry" attitude.

Once reaching the first tee, Hogan would be just as careful to give himself every advantage. Reading what he said to Nick Seitz, the interviewer for *Golf Digest*, will help you understand how course-smart Hogan was:

"They would call out our names, and I would take longer on that first tee than I would any other place on the golf course," said Hogan.

"I was gearing my brain. Taking a look at that fairway. Taking three or four practice swings. A lot of people wondered what I was doing up there. Why I didn't tee the ball up and hit it. I was organizing myself to play this round. I thought harder about that first shot than any shot I played. It set the tone for the day."

Out on the course, Hogan was a superb course manager. The fade he hit off the tee allowed him to start the ball down the left side of the fairway and work back to the middle. This was a smart strategy because even if the ball failed to drift enough to the right, it was still on the short grass. Also, if the left-to-right shot sliced, it would still finish on the right side of the fairway. The fade was such a high percentage shot that, unless the hole turned sharply left and forced Hogan to play a soft draw, he would go with his old reliable left-to-right strategy.

Hogan was eccentric, yes, but his impeccable preparation contributed to his winning ways. Hogan once turned to Sam Snead and said, "All I care about when I'm on the course is hitting the ball from point A to point B, sticking to a game plan and staying focused." According to Snead, Hogan was never one to walk along the gallery ropes and shake hands with friends and fans, say hello, or even nod to acknowledge their presence. On the course, during competition, Hogan truly was all business. According to Jules Alexander, the famous photographer who started shooting pictures of Hogan at New York's Winged Foot Golf Club during the 1959 U.S. Open, "Hogan concentrated so hard you could see the thoughts on his forehead."

Hogan's secret to playing winning golf was making as few mistakes as possible and never allowing himself to get upset. After blowing the 1952 U.S. Open, Hogan told famous sports writer and author Dan Jenkins: "Golf is a game of mistakes. I made too many and let some of them bother me. You can't do that."

Hogan was so mindful of everything that affected his game positively that he even paid close attention to his clothes. Cotton shirts in conservative colors, professionally tailored perfectly creased trousers, cashmere sweaters, white or black leather shoes boasting a military gloss, and a white cap from Cavanaugh, raised Hogan's level of confidence.

Over time, Hogan learned that certain sounds hurt his performance, namely the rustling sounds of a moving gallery or the click of a camera. So he chose to enter a mental cocoon of concentration, and stayed on his psychic path until the round was over.

Just as it took Hogan years to develop a swing that he could depend on, it took him even longer to realize that there is an art to "going low." That art depends on a knowledge of equipment, common sense, perception, an awareness of the weather conditions, patience, a knowledge of the course and the conditions of the fairways and greens, and the ability to stay levelheaded when shooting a low or high score on a hole.

"Hogan learned to understand the many elements to good scoring so well that he was in a class of his own," said Tiger Woods's coach Butch Harmon, who learned many things from playing just one round with Hogan. "He never hit a shot before he had carefully planned it out. He never hit a shot before he visualized the ball flying on a particular line. He rarely missed his target."

Hogan's contemporaries, certainly Byron Nelson, studied the game but not with the same passion. Hogan's appetite for improvement was so big that he never stopped thinking about strategies that would enable him to swing more proficiently and cut strokes off his score. He was so fanatical that he studied the soles of golf shoes. He came to the conclusion that footwear manufacturers failed to include a spike in the ball area of the right shoe that would aid in balance and provide a way to push off the right foot during the downswing, with no fear of slipping and losing power. Hogan had a spike added and his swing improved.

Another adjustment Hogan made that even many of

his most enthusiastic fans are not aware of is having his 3-wood be the same length as his driver. By lengthening the 3-wood to 43.5 inches, the radius formed by the left arm and the clubshaft grew longer. Consequently, the arc of his swing became larger, which helped create more power. This was a big advantage. Hogan's fellow players may have been smart enough to play a safe tee shot on a narrow par-4 hole with a 3-wood, but because their club was standard length they could not hit the ball as far as Hogan. More length off the tee meant a shorter approach into the green, employing a more lofted club that was easier to control. Hogan took advantage of this and often birdied these narrow holes.

Hogan was so clever he had fairly flat reminder grips on his clubs that encouraged him to keep his hands more on top of the handle, in a weak position with the thumbs pointing straight down the handle. He also had a string built into the grips that pointed straight down the shaft. This innovative feature further helped him hold the club with a weak grip and work the ball from left to right. Hogan's hands were quite large, too, so he had the grips of his clubs built up to alleviate any looseness that could cause the hands-arms-club release to be exaggerated, the clubface to close at impact, or the ball to hook. Hogan kept his hands fairly low at address, which is why he had his clubs tailored so they sat on a flatter angle than normal. Hogan's clubs also featured the stiffest shafts available, especially since they were tipped at the end. I've heard from more than one source that even power-hitter Mike Souchak, who was a hulk of

**H**ogan took his time selecting a club. But once he made a decision, he cast his eyes coldly on the target to get a feel for the shot he was about to play.

a man, could not swing them. Hogan did not want any "play" in the shaft because he felt this feature encouraged a hook shot, which was his nemesis.

In preparing to play approach shots Hogan depended mostly on the reliability of his eyes to judge distance, as did Bobby Jones before him. Hogan was not big on carrying a memo pad containing drawings of each hole that showed the lurking hazards, various pin placements, and distances to specific parts of the green. Hogan made mental notes of the course during practice rounds. One thing was certain about Hogan: he would take his time to choose a club, but once he made his choice he stuck to it, then began staring down his target.

Hogan was very savvy about club selection because he knew so much about his shotmaking game and about himself. By hitting thousands of balls and recording data, he knew the average distance he hit each club in his bag. He hit the driver an average distance of 260 yards, the 3-wood, 235 yards. His 1-iron traveled a distance of 220 yards; 2-iron, 210 yards; 3-iron, 200 yards; 4-iron, 190 yards; 5-iron, 180 yards; 6-iron, 170 yards; 7-iron, 160 yards; 8-iron, 150 yards; 9-iron, 140 yards; pitching wedge, 120 yards; and sand wedge, 100 yards. Hogan was smarter than the rest of his contemporaries. He had really done his homework. He knew he hit the ball an average of ten yards longer when he was pumped up or when he faced a flyer lie. He knew he hit the ball ten yards shorter when he was tired.

Most often, when playing an approach, Hogan aimed at the middle of the green and hit a power-fade shot.

And at times, he was even more conservative. On occasion, he purposely missed a green, which surprised other players who didn't understand the method to his apparent madness. For example, if the pin were placed in the very front of a steeply pitched, lightning-fast, two-tier green, Hogan often would hit into a bunker situated in front of it. He figured it was easier to get the ball down in two strokes from a bunker than when putting from say 30 feet above the hole. In stroking the putt down a steep slope, Hogan knew that there was a good chance of three-putting, regardless of his good lag-putting skills.

Hogan was so much smarter than his fellow players that he would aim for fringe grass on the right side of hole number 11 at Augusta National to avoid a water hazard that lurks on the left side of the green. From the fringe, Hogan would usually score par. A shot hit in the "drink" usually lead to a double bogie.

Hogan rarely hit the ball directly at the flag. In fact, if he hit the flagstick it was an accident. To him, a smarter and safer strategy was to aim for the middle of the green, or a position on the putting surface that would leave him an uphill putt.

Only when Hogan was in contention in a tournament, and in need of a birdie down the stretch of the final round, did he become a little more aggressive. If the pin was on the left side of the green, he would hit the ball toward the fringe on that side and let the shot work back toward the hole. If the pin were on the right portion of the green, he would start the shot at its center and work the ball back to the hole.

After swinging into a high finish (above), Hogan quietly pulled the club down and analyzed the flight of the ball (right).

Before deciding when to attack a tough pin position, Hogan always took the shot situation as well as his own shotmaking strategies into account. He never tried to play miracle shots. Heed his strategy. If you're a high handicapper and don't have a lot of confidence in your iron play, don't challenge a tough pin. Your best bet is to try to land the ball in the middle of the green every time. If you are a low handicapper, you obviously have more options to consider. For a short-iron shot, you may be able to hit the ball high and soft enough that it's reasonable to go for the pin. But if it's a long-iron shot you face, the smart play may be to shade toward the middle of the green. Another factor is where the pin is positioned. If it's tucked left and you draw the ball with confidence, you can play an attacking shot. If you fade your irons, play for the fat part of the green. Finally, always go with your instincts. If you have doubts about going for a tightly tucked pin, those doubts will probably be reflected in your swing. Take a lesson from Hogan: Plan a shot that you are 100 percent confident you can hit.

One chief reason why Hogan was such a controlled iron player was the shortness of his swing. Normally, he swung the club back to the three-quarter point and stopped. Making the same compact backswing will keep you centered over the ball and enable you to better time the movements of the club on the downswing.

Part of Hogan's on-course strategy was to swing into a high finish position, quietly pull the club back down, then watch how the ball reacted in the air and on the ground. During a serious competition, Hogan followed the ball intently with his eyes to track any variances in ball flight that indicated a swing problem, or the start of one. If Hogan could not stop a fade from moving a little too much from left to right in the air, he would make adjustments in aim and ball position during play, then work to find the root cause and a cure during postround practice.

Between shots, Hogan liked to look at what shot he faced next, then mentally rehearse the swing he would need to hit that shot. Hogan believed that his body was better able to find a way to perform the necessary muscular swing movements when he had a clear picture of the intended shot in his mind.

While walking to the ball after swinging, Hogan did something that was very unique, or rather eccentric. Instead of letting his caddy put the club back in the bag, he would often walk down the fairway holding it, in order to keep himself connected to the game. Mostly, he did this during major championships because he did not want to give himself any opportunity to lose concentration.

In hitting wedge shots from a slightly open stance, Hogan stared at the top of the flagstick rather than at the middle of it, as most pros and amateurs do. This unique strategy encouraged him to hit the ball to the hole. If you come up short of the hole on wedge shots, try mimicking the master.

When playing the first bunker shot of the round, Hogan listened to the sound the bounce of the club made when it contacted the sand. This strategy allowed

**A**fter Hogan played a shot, he often kept hold of the club until he arrived at the ball to play his next shot. This strategy will help you stay in the game mentally.

Hogan to get a sense of the sand's texture. If there was a sort of thud at impact, this signaled firmer sand and told Hogan he should hit down more softly. If the club-to-sand sound was closer to a swish, Hogan knew the sand was soft and he would need to hit down and through more swiftly.

On the greens, Hogan squatted behind the ball to get a bird's-eye view of the line. He remained in that position until he visualized the ball rolling along a particular line and dropping into the hole.

When it came his turn to putt, Hogan sometimes stunned his fellow stroke-play competitors by asking for the pin to be tended from 15 feet and over. Through experimental practice, he found this helped his perception, thereby encouraging better distance control. Hogan varied his putting strokes, too. On short putts, he employed a short hit-and-hold action. On long putts, he made the same short backswing, but accelerated the putter through using a pushing action. On all putts, Hogan did something very unique. He laid the putter down in front of the ball then behind it before starting the stroke with a forward press. Look for something personal to help you become a more confident player on the greens.

Hogan was a die putter. He believed the ball had a better chance of falling into the cup if it was rolled slowly across the green.

On par-three holes, Hogan teed the ball up to alleviate any chance of hitting a flyer. Hogan also believed that teeing the ball off the ground helped him hit a

**W**hen blasting out of a bunker, early in the round, Hogan listened to the sound of impact. This strategy enabled him to learn about the texture of the sand.

higher, soft-landing shot, and thus play more aggressively at the flag provided the risk was worth it. Depending on the type of club Hogan had in his hand, and the shot he planned to play, he would tee the ball up in different ways. On short-iron shots, he teed the ball up just above the grass or about one-quarter inch in height. For long-iron tee shots, he teed the ball about a half-inch off the ground. For a low driving shot, he tipped the tee forward slightly. When wanting to play a high soft shot, say playing downwind or to a tight pin, Hogan tilted the tee back slightly to encourage a clean upswing hit.

On par-four and par-five holes, Hogan never took silly chances. Unless the rewards far outweighed the risk, he would not think of "shortening" the hole by hooking or slicing the ball around the corner. He simply put the ball in play, hitting his trusty power-fade shot off the tee. He would not try to drive a short par-4 or go for a par-5 in two, either, unless the conditions of wind and terrain were just right, he was swinging exceptionally well, and he needed to go for broke.

On windy days, Hogan used his noggin well, which explains why he won the British Open the first and only time he competed in the prestigious championship. Hogan believed that the best strategy when hitting into wind was to swing more smoothly. The slower swing helps you maintain good balance and stay in control of the club. Hogan also selected one extra club for every ten miles per hour of wind. For example, Hogan would select a 7-iron instead of a 9-iron when hitting an approach shot into a 20-miles-per-hour wind.

**W**hen putting from 15 feet and over, Hogan often had the flag tended by his caddy in order to help his depth perception.

When playing drives downwind, Hogan usually positioned the ball more forward in the stance, so he could hit a higher shot and take advantage of the conditions. On downwind iron shots, he normally played the ball back in his stance, and played under the wind to avoid overshooting the green.

In a right-to-left crosswind, Hogan preferred fading the ball into it. In a left-to-right crosswind, he did not hook the ball into it, like most of his contemporaries. He avoided the shot at all costs. He simply aimed further left, swung normally, and let the wind drift the ball back to the fairway.

Hogan's intelligent strategies were not limited to stroke-play competition. In match-play events he proved to be a very intimidating opponent, due to his confident attitude, flawless swing, and strong strategic mind.

When going up against an opponent, Hogan did not chitchat on the first tee. He waited for his opponent to say "good luck," then merely nodded. He was in his own world, like some boxers before a championship bout. During the match, he kept a straight face. No matter whether he hit a good shot or a bad shot, scored birdie or bogie, he never let his opponent know what he was thinking.

In preparing to play his first shot of the day, Hogan took extra time, particularly if he had the honor. Hogan knew that if he hit a good shot it would put pressure on his opponent and maybe force an error. Winning the first hole was also important to Hogan, because he figured his opponent would start feeling he had to play catch-up and might start making silly mistakes, like attacking a "sucker pin" tucked behind water or a deep bunker.

Hogan competed against the course more than against his opponent, knowing that if he kept hitting fairways off the tee and greens in regulation figures, and putted halfway decently, his adversary would have little chance of winning.

Hogan's play on the course was very much like that of Willie Mosconi on the pool table. Just as Mosconi thought about positioning the cue ball in the most strategic spot to play his next shot, Hogan always played for position. Hogan never rushed, either. He stuck to his same methodical routine, no matter how fast his opponent played. Hogan was a master strategist who was reputed to preplan his rounds on a blackboard in his hotel room every evening prior to a championship round.

Around the greens, and on them, he was smart, too. Hogan was so into playing the course that he did not change his game plan because of a shot an opponent hit. He never putted or chipped aggressively, unless he knew the percentages for holing out were in his favor.

Mentally, Hogan was the toughest around. He had overcome such adversity in his life that being down in a match did not bother him. Hogan knew that if he stuck to his game plan and made a birdie or two, his opponent would fold. When he was up in a match, he tried to get further up. Hogan possessed a quiet killer instinct common to all good match players. And it worked wonders, as his Ryder Cup record attests. Hogan played for the

On the course, during tournament play, Hogan minded his own business. He had no time for small talk, since his goals were to play to the best of his ability, give every shot 100 percent concentration, and finish first.

American squad in 1941, 1947, and 1951 against Great Britain and Ireland's best golfers, and never lost a match.

Hogan's strongest suits as a strategist revolved around care and caution. He always examined the lie carefully, as well as considering the wind direction and the firmness or softness of the green and its surrounding terrain. Hogan was so cautious that he never tried to hit the miracle shot. He knew his capabilities and always played within himself. He never tried to make up for lost ground by attacking a flag that was close to trouble. Like a great military general with materiel and manpower at his disposal, Hogan's unsurpassed swing would let him execute his game plan and win the battle, against the course in medal play and against an opponent in match play.

# Index

# INDEX